IDEApreneur

How to Turn Ideas into Income and
Make Money from Your Mind

By Sam Horn,

Author of **POP!**, **Tongue Fu!**® and
Got Your Attention?

IDEApreneur: How to Turn Ideas into Income and Make Money from Your Mind

Copyright © 2016 Sam Horn

www.IntrigueAgency.com

All rights reserved. No part of this book may be reproduced in any form or by any electronic or mechanical means, including information storage and retrieval systems, without written permission from the author, except in the case of a reviewer, who may quote brief passages embodied in critical articles or in a review.

Trademarked names may appear throughout this book. Rather than use a trademark symbol with every occurrence of a trademarked name, names are used in an editorial fashion, with no intention of infringement of the respective owner's trademark.

The information in this book is distributed on an "as is" basis, without warranty. Although every precaution has been taken in the preparation of this work, neither the author nor the publisher shall have any liability to any person or entity with respect to any loss or damage caused or alleged to be caused directly or indirectly by the information contained in this book.

ISBN 978-1629671642

TABLE OF CONTENTS

Introduction 1

Section 1: Ready to Become an IDEApreneur? 3
    Chapter 1: What's The Big Idea? 5
    Chapter 2: They Don't Call Them Fleeting
        Thoughts for Nothing 11
    Chapter 3: Find Your Third Place 19
    Chapter 4: Create Real-Life Ideas by Connecting
        with Real-Life People 23
    Chapter 5: Where Do You Get Your Ideas? 31
    Chapter 6: Attain, Sustain and Regain the IDEA Zone 37

**Section II: Complete Your W-5 Form So Your Ideas Are
Commercially Viable** 57
    Chapter 7: Assess Your I.D.E.A. for Equity Potential 59
    Chapter 8: Complete a W5 Form to Make Your Idea
        a Mutual ROI 67
    Chapter 9: Identify Your P.O.D (Points of Distinction) 75

Section III: Turn Ordinary Ideas into One-of-a-Kind Ideas .. 83
    Chapter 10: Turn Your Idea into a Trademark-able Term 85
    Chapter 11: Create the Next New Thing by
        Combining the Best of Two Ideas 95
    Chapter 12: The Secret to Turning Generic Ideas
        into Genius Ideas 101

Section IV: Make Your Ideas Marketable and Memorable 109
    Chapter 13: Re-arrange Clichés to Give Your Idea
        a Fresh Twist 111
    Chapter 14: Make Your Idea Relatable 115
    Chapter 15: Craft a Tell 'n Sell Elevator Pitch for Your Idea ... 119
    Chapter 16: Use True Humor to Win Buy-In for Your Idea ... 127
    Chapter 17: Make Your Idea Sing and Swing 137

Section V: Monetize Your Ideas with Ongoing Business Activities 145

Chapter 18: Be the Master of Your Idea's Domain 147
Chapter 19: Merchandise Ideas by Turning Them
  into Images and Icons 155
Chapter 20: Become a Topic Expert Who Gets
  Paid to Speak 161
Chapter 21: Get Paid to Consult/Coach on Your Idea 179
Chapter 22: Get Paid to Write on Your Idea 187
Chapter 23: Get Interviewed by Media on Your Idea 197
Chapter 24: Scale Your Idea's Visibility Via
  Strategic Social Media 205

Section VI: Ensure Ongoing Success 215

Chapter 25: Set-up an IDEA Accountability Group
  for Support, Synergy and Results 217
Chapter 26: Act on Your Ideas to Scale Your
  Influence and Income – for Good 229

About the Author: Sam Horn 239

Want to Work with Sam? 242

INTRODUCTION

"No matter what people tell you, words and ideas can change the world."
– Robin Williams

WELCOME. Congratulations to you for carving time out of your busy schedule to discover how to make a mint from your mind. I agree with Robin Williams that words and ideas can change the world and your world for good.

If your goal is to produce one-of-a-kind ideas you can monetize, you're in the right place.

You're about to discover how to generate commercially-viable ideas (what I call "equity ideas") that are so interesting, unique and bottom-line beneficial, people will gladly pay for them. Most importantly, you'll learn how to act on your ideas and turn them into income.

The premise of this book and my approach to this topic is that ideas in our head help no one. Ideas themselves don't have the power to change the world and become a profitable reality until we turn them into a tangible product, service or business.

That's why this book provides you with a step-by-step SYSTEM on how to become an IDEApreneur who consciously and strategically:

a. increases your flow of ideas
b. assesses your ideas for uniqueness and money-making potential
c. positions, packages and communicates your ideas so they get noticed, respected and bought
d. markets, merchandises, monetizes your ideas through a variety of strategic business activities

Sam Horn

Best-selling author Kurt Vonnegut was asked, "What's the secret to writing a great book?" He thought about it for a moment and then said, "You've got to be a good date for the reader." My goal is to be a good date for you.

I promise not to waste time on abstract theories that don't work in the real world. You're about to learn proven techniques and tools you can use immediately to generate marketable, memorable, merchandisable ideas that get noticed and get bought.

Ready to get started?

Read on!

SECTION I
Ready To Become An IDEApreneur?

"Time is long, but life is short."
– Stevie Wonder

STEVIE IS RIGHT. Life is short and thinking small is a waste of time and talent.

Why not think big? Why not learn how to leverage time by thinking up equity ideas that can make a positive difference for others and a prosperous living for you?

This first section shows you how to become an IDEApreneur so, for the rest of your life, you're capitalizing on your mind's gifts instead of taking them for granted and throwing away their money-making, difference-making potential.

CHAPTER 1
What's The Big Idea?

"Ideas are the beginning points of all fortunes."
– Napoleon Hill

THE PURPOSE of this chapter is to convince you that ideas aren't frivolous; they can, as Napoleon Hill pointed out, be the fount of good fortune, your pathway to prosperity.

Instead of ignoring ideas and telling yourself, "Yeah, it's a good idea, but I'm not an entrepreneur," or "I don't have a degree or educational background in this," or "I don't have any money to invest in this," please understand that **ideas believe in equal opportunity**.

Big ideas don't discriminate. They can occur to anyone: teens, teachers, stay-at-home moms, CEO's, attorneys, taxi drivers.

The question is, **do you ACT on your big idea or do you let it slip through your mental fingers?**

As you're about to find out, anyone can profit from a big idea if you evaluate its viability, draft a strategic plan to turn it into reality, and persevere until you produce profitability.

Please read this book with pen in hand (or a highlighter on your e-reader) and take notes on how you plan to apply these step-by-step instructions to turn YOUR big idea into a profitable reality.

I'll always remember my first "big idea."

We had just returned from an old-fashioned family Christmas reuniting with cousins, aunts and uncles at "Granny's house" in Eagle Rock, CA. We ate the traditional turkey dinner with stuffing, mashed potatoes, Granny's gravy (none better), and her special overnight fruit salad with home-made whipped cream. Obviously, this was before anyone cared about counting carbs.

We arrived home after 3 days away to find our poor Dalmatian dog Tres (three spots on the top of his head) dehydrated and starving. The neighbor we had asked to watch him had left town in an emergency and forgot to ask someone else to take care of him.

For months afterwards, I felt terribly guilty that we had left our dog with no food or water. I remember waking up in the middle of the night with an idea. Why not design a contraption that "metered" out water and food every day so we could be sure our beloved pet was taken care of while we were away?

I couldn't get the idea out of my head. It just made so much sense. I envisioned millions of people (and their pets) benefiting from this backup plan.

I never did anything about it though. I was "just a kid" after all. What did I know about inventing something? I didn't even tell anyone my idea because I was afraid they'd laugh at me. Furthermore, I rationalized, if it was such a good idea, someone would have already thought of it, right?

Imagine my dismay when I was leafing through a mail order catalog in my teens and, there it was, a device that portioned out food and water for pets. Someone else made a fortune because they talked themselves *into* acting on that idea … while I had talked myself *out* of it.

Years later, I had another bright idea. I swam competitively growing up in California, both in our community's summer league and for my high school.

Upon moving to Hawaii in the early 80's, I participated in Oahu's annual 2.4-mile Rough Water Swim, held off Waikiki Beach every Labor Day.

I thoroughly enjoyed training in the ocean at Ala Moana Beach Park. Then, we moved to a Honolulu high-rise which had one of those tiny apartment pools. It was frustrating getting my daily mile in because the pool was so small. Stroke, stroke, turn. Stroke, stroke, turn. It took all the fun out of swimming and I started skipping training workouts.

I woke up one night (by the way, there's a reason we often have ideas in the middle of the night and it's explained in Chapter 6) and wondered, "Why not design a swim leash so I could tie myself to the end of the pool and churn away to my heart's content without having to stop and do a flip turn every few seconds?"

Many serious swimmers stop using their backyard pools because it's an "exercise in frustration" (so to speak) doing laps in them. The "Swim Leash" made it possible to get lost in that athletic reverie, that blissful ZONE, in which your mind switches to automatic pilot and you're no longer thinking about the stitch in your side, the cramp in your legs, or the ache in your arms.

I made up a makeshift one, shaping a "belt" from the rubber fabric of a wet-suit, a couple of D rings, and a length of water-proof boat rope. I got in the pool, tied myself to the entrance ladder and started swimming. IT WORKED!

Furthermore, the "Swim Leash" worked with every stroke, including my favorite, the backstroke. I loved looking up at the sky (instead of the bottom of the pool), watching birds fly by and letting my mind wander while I got a vigorous workout.

After testing the prototype, I went to an "invention convention" full of hope and dreams ... and promptly got overwhelmed. Several experts agreed it was viable, but told me I'd have to manufacture it overseas since labor costs in Hawaii were so high. Plus, they said I'd need to hire a lawyer to handle the patent process, obtain venture capital, locate suppliers, purchase liability insurance etc.

Bummer.

I had two small sons (Tom and Andrew, now thriving adults) and an active career as a professional speaker. Who had the time or resources to fly overseas and put all this together? I reluctantly concluded I wasn't in a position to pursue this and put the project on the shelf (literally and figuratively).

Years later I was flying to keynote a convention, pulled out a copy of *SkyMall* from the seat pocket in front of me, started leafing through it … and there was "*my*" invention. It wasn't called a swim leash, but it was a similar idea.

SkyMall also advertised a $4500 one-person "pool" with an artificial current where you swam in place. I tried it at a hotel spa and found it difficult and uncomfortable to use. First, it's like swimming in rough seas because you have water coming into your mouth with force. Second, you have to swim at a constant speed or you end up bumping into the back of the pool. It would have been a real drag to pay $4500 only to discover that idea worked better in theory than in practice.

Once again, I wished I had pursued my big ideas instead of abandoning them.

Oh well, too late for remorse. The only thing I can do now is to *act* on my money-making ideas.

Has this happened to you? Have you come up with a bright idea, got all excited, and started researching it, only to get discouraged and distracted along the way, eventually dropping the project altogether?

No more.

The internet has changed everything. Whether you have an idea for a business, product or service, you can turn it into a profitable reality in a fraction of the time and money it used to cost.

You're about to learn how to take your ideas and turn them into income. And the good news is, you don't have to have an MBA to do this. In fact, Oprah Winfrey featured a 13-year-old girl (and her MOMpreneur) on her show who turned a casual idea into a million-dollar company.

Are you familiar with the brightly colored plastic shoes called Crocs?

They themselves are an Equity Idea that were "thought up" by a man who was given a pair of boat shoes to wear while sailing. As he walked safely around the slippery deck, he thought, "Gee, these are comfortable, they offer good arch support, they're inexpensive, they don't get ruined when they're wet and they could be mass-produced." He acted on his Equity Idea and the rest is, as they say, pop culture history.

Back to the 13-year-old girl. She and her friends had a sleepover and had fun "dressing up" their Crocs with charms, earrings and baubles from her mom's jewelry box. Her mother saw what they'd done and thought, "Hmmm, why don't we make little Croc ornaments? We could put them into the holes of our Crocs to personalize them, kind of like a charm bracelet for your feet."

Not content to just ponder the idea's potential, the two started a small business, reserved a booth at a local craft show and sold out their first batch of inventory. They eventually came to the attention of Oprah's producers who asked them to appear on her TV show. The result? A "casual" idea that has resulted in a multi-million-dollar company.

Chances are, you have high-potential ideas too. Why not profit from them?

Anne Frank said, "How wonderful it is that nobody need wait a single moment before starting to improve the world."

From now on, don't wait a single moment to act on the ideas that occur to you all day, every day.

If you use the techniques in the book, who knows, maybe we'll see you on Oprah, sharing your idea with the world.

Questions to Ask – Actions to Take

1. Have you had a big idea before? Did you talk yourself into it or out of it? What happened?
2. Who is an IDEApreneur you respect? Who is someone you saw on Shark Tank, QVC or Home Shopping Channel who turned their idea into a fortune?

CHAPTER 2
They Don't Call Them Fleeting Thoughts For Nothing

"Time is the coin of your life. It is the only coin you have and only you can determine how it will be spent. Be careful lest you let other people spend it for you."
– Carl Sandburg

TIME MAY BE THE COIN of our life, but *ideas* **are the coins of our future. All too frequently, though, we let ideas slip through our mental fingers. We think we'll remember them later, but we don't. They don't call them fleeting thoughts for nothing**.

Were you one of those inquisitive kids who was always asking "*Why?*"

Did the significant others in your life – parents, teachers, friends and extended family members – take the time to answer your questions? Did they encourage your curiosity and creativity?

If so, kudos to them for fostering and supporting your IDEApreneur imagination. Unfortunately, a lot of people had their imagination, curiosity and creativity squashed in their early years.

One woman I interviewed told me, "Do you know what I heard growing up? 'Curiosity killed the cat,' 'Children are to be seen, not heard,' 'You're driving me crazy with all these questions.'"

Yikes. What type of subliminal (or not so subliminal) messaging have you gotten along the way about the merits (or lack of merits) of being imaginative, full of curiosity and creativity?

If you were repeatedly told "Stick to the assignment" or "Stop wool-gathering," or "You're imagining things again," you may be harboring a block against ideas without even realizing it.

You may be squelching your curiosity and creativity (which are like the chicken and the egg) because you were taught early on it was unproductive, frivolous, a waste of time.

I was talking about this often unintentional negative programming with my walking buddy, and she literally stopped in her tracks and looked at me in astonishment and said, "Do you know what I was told all through school? 'Stop daydreaming. Get your head out of the clouds.'"

What lingering negative connotations might you have related to ideas, curiosity and creativity?

If we were to play word association right now, what are the first words that come to mind when you hear the words "imagination," "creativity" and "curiosity?"

Do you feel ideas are fun but ultimately frivolous because they "won't pay the bills?" When you get an idea, do you go "Hmmm," but then move on because you think "I have more important things to do?" or "That will never amount to anything?"

If you are wondering, "Why are you emphasizing this, Sam?" it's because I've observed, after two decades of speaking, writing and consulting about this topic, that many people have unfavorable "stigmas" regarding their imagination. As a result, they have a habit of automatically rejecting new ideas, a default of dismissing them with rolled eyes.

Charles Brower, the CEO of an ad agency, said, "Ideas are delicate. They can be killed by a sneer or a yawn; they can be stabbed to death by a quip and worried to death by a frown."

As stated before, the purpose of this chapter is to convince you that ideas aren't frivolous; they can be the fount of good fortune, your pathway to prosperity.

Instead of dismissing ideas as an indulgent distraction, telling yourself you'll explore them when you have more time, (face it, we'll never have more time than we have right now), or letting people kill them with a sneer, yawn or frown . . . please understand you can make a *good* living (literally and figuratively) by capturing your ideas and turning them into income.

Starting today, if your mind starts wondering, understand it is not wandering. It is breaking new ground, charting a new path.

When you wonder, "Why do we always do it this way? Why don't we do it a different way? How could we do this a better way?" your imagination is in the process of innovation.

Carry on. In fact, don't just carry on, use these Three A's to Capture Fleeting Thoughts Before They Escape.

Three A's to Capture Fleeting Thoughts Before They Escape

A = Appreciate

The first step is to appreciate that ideas are a gift. Think about it. Many ideas just show up in your head, seemingly out of nowhere. One minute they're not there, the next minute they are.

Yet, many times we ignore vs. explore an idea's potential. We table it ("I don't have time") or diminish it ("That's silly") or don't even notice it ("What idea?"). We promise ourselves we'll remember it later (wrong). The vast majority of us treat ideas way too casually.

We don't seem to appreciate that these "gleams of light which flash across the mind from within" (which is what Ralph Waldo Emerson called ideas) are a modern-day dowry, bringing the potential of a fortune if we just take the time to explore them.

When ideas appear, they're often imperfect. By definition, they are new and not thought through, so there are things wrong with them. If we immediately criticize them and focusing on what's wrong, we're sure to find loopholes and impracticalities.

Henry David Thoreau said, "The fault-finder will find faults even in paradise. Love your life."

The same is true with ideas. If you seek fault, you'll find it. Instead of focusing first on what's *wrong* with an idea, focus on what's *right* with it. Instead of immediately pointing out its problems, explore its potential. It's important to love fragile ideas from the beginning so they have a chance to flourish. Embrace them so they feel comfortable poking their baby heads out. Welcome them into the world. There you are!

No criticizing or condemning allowed in the beginning. You can determine whether the idea is practical and feasible AFTER you invite it to stay (and play) in your mental home for a while.

An IDEApreneurial mantra is: "Appreciate ideas first, evaluate them next."

A = Alert

Once we appreciate that every idea has the potential to change our life (and the lives of others) for the better, we're more motivated to stay alert and keep our antenna up for them.

In particular, be alert for, and pay attention to, *the thoughts we can't get out of our head.*

That's a sure sign an idea wants to be born. It is knock, knock, knocking at our mental door, pleading, "Let me in. Notice me. I come bearing gifts."

Popular musician Billy Joel has learned the power of capturing ideas he can't get out of his head. Joel was being interviewed on *CBS Sunday Morning*. The reporter asked, "How do you create the lyrics to such classics as *The Piano Man* and *New York State of Mind?*"

Joel said lyrics often "come to him" while working on his hobby which is designing and building boats. "Working with my hands frees up my head," he said, "and musical phrases often pop into my mind. One time, the line 'In the middle of the night, I was walking through my sleep" came to me. I thought, 'Naw, that's too simple,' rejected it, and went back to working on the boat.

"I went to take a shower to clean up and found myself humming a tune to that lyric. I couldn't get it out of my mind. So, I wrote it down despite thinking it wouldn't amount to much."

You probably know the rest of that story. That line evolved into *River of Dreams*, one of Joel's 40 chart-topping songs. Imagine if he hadn't followed up on that tune he couldn't stop thinking about? Imagine if he had ignored the muse and talked himself out of a platinum selling record?

Yet many of us do a version of that every day. We talk ourselves out of potential moneymaking ideas by not being alert to them and by not honoring the muse and our intuitive instincts.

Please reframe your mental picture of what idea generation looks like. It is NOT something that only happens when sitting around a table brainstorming or when working at your desk or on your laptop. It is something that happens on planes, while waiting in line at the post office, while taking a shower, and as Billy Joel pointed out, in the middle of the night.

Instead of getting annoyed with ideas you "can't get out of our mind," understand they're persistently knocking at your mental door. That means they have potential – and it's up to you to explore them to see if they could become a profitable reality. That idea could be a windfall – a secure financial future – staring you in the face.

A = Act

The first two steps are important to capturing ideas so they don't escape *in the moment* – this third step keeps them from escaping *over time*. In fact, if we don't record an idea the instant it occurs to us, we really can't claim we're doing the first two steps.

I'll always be indebted to former National Geographic photographer Dewitt Jones for teaching me this. Dewitt models how a one-of-a-kind idea can result in a rewarding, profitable career where we make a good living from our mind ... *for decades.*

Dewitt's novel idea was this. Why not use his stunning photographs as before-and-after metaphors for life lessons? For example, one photo in his stunning slide deck shows an aweinspiring waterfall tumbling down the face of a desolate rocky cliff. The audience oohs and aahs.

His next photograph zooms in on a tiny portion of the previous picture. To the audience's surprise, a scraggly little tree is somehow jutting out horizontally from the cliff-face next to the waterfall. The audience gasps in astonishment.

Dewitt then points out that sometimes we give things a cursory look and think we've seen it all when, in reality, we're overlooking something that could add value. He says sometimes we look at the world with a "wide-angle" lens and it can be advantageous to switch to a telephoto lens and examine things more closely. It's a profound, provocative reminder to look at issues from difference angles so we don't miss small but important details. His presentation is packed with other such epiphanies, all aided by visual juxtaposition of before-and-after photos.

Dewitt, (who lives part-time in Hawaii) and I were enjoying a walk/talk along a Maui beach. We were having a great time discussing the fascinating topic of intuition. What is intuition? Where does it come from? Why is it never wrong? How can we capitalize on it?

Dewitt was doing something that puzzled me. We would go about 100 yards and he would stop, whip out a little notebook and pen from his pocket and write something down. We'd go another couple hundred yards and Dewitt would stop again and scribble something down. He kept doing this until I finally asked, "Dewitt, what are you doing?"

He said, "Sam, I used to get ideas and think, 'That'd be an interesting topic for my next column,' or 'I've got to include that in my presentation tomorrow,' but then I'd get caught up in other things and forget all about it. I finally realized, "I make my living from my mind. I started carrying a notebook with me everywhere I go to capture ideas. It's part of my profession now." How many times have you gotten an idea and then gone about your day and forgotten it?

If there's anything I've learned in twenty years of researching, writing and speaking about innovation, it's that *this* is how our best ideas come to us ... they pop into our mind. And if we don't write them down as they occur, they're gone ... *out-of-sight, out-of-mind*.

What's worse, if we allow our inner critic to kick in and tell us all the reasons this idea won't work, we 'diss the muse ... and she gets ticked. She thinks, "I'm giving you gold here. If you don't want it, I'm out of here. I'll go find someone who appreciates me."

From now on, realize that if you want to make your living from your mind, you need to record ideas and sudden insights in a notebook you carry with you everywhere you go.

Carry a digital recorder, use Voice Recorder on your cell phone, call yourself and leave a message, DO SOMETHING to capture ideas before they flee, gone forever. You may not know where this idea or insight fits into your work. Just trust that it will.

Our greatest minds, from Einstein to Ralph Waldo Emerson to Mozart, have understood and honored the power of the "muse." As Emerson said, "Look sharply after your thoughts. They come unlooked for, like a new bird seen in your trees, and, if you turn to your usual task, disappear." These thought leaders knew if they were fortunate enough to be gifted with a revelation, it was their job to write it down. If they didn't, it was gone.

I call this, "Muse it or lose it." If you take a moment to jot thoughts when they're hot, they will be there waiting for you, days, months, years later when you're ready for them. You will have captured those fleeting thoughts instead of them disappearing back to where they come from.

Questions to Ask – Actions to Take

1. How will you capture fleeting thoughts before they have a chance to escape? How will you be more alert to the ideas, insights and observations popping into your head?
2. How will you up your appreciation for ideas? How will you see them as the gift they are and be more present and grateful for these mental presents?
3. How will you act on your ideas? Will you muse them so you don't lose them? Ink them when you think them? Will you keep an idea journal handy? Record them on your digital device?

CHAPTER 3
Find Your Third Place

"My husband told me he wanted more space, so I locked him outside." – **Roseanne Barr**

DO YOU HAVE a designated place where you brainstorm ideas and do creative work? Do you, as Virginia Woolf suggested, have a "room of your own" to write, paint, compose, sketch or invent?

Authors, artists, sculptors and other creative types have come to understand that having a dedicated work space plays a pivotal role in their ability to make steady progress.

Ron Culbertson, a friend and former President of National Speakers Association, worked from his home office and was also active in his local Rotary club and with his kids' sports teams. Ron found it almost impossible to work on his book while juggling all his different obligations.

"Between the phone calls, emails, paperwork, and questions from my wife and kids, it seemed like I was being interrupted every 10 minutes."

Sound familiar? If interruptions and distractions are undermining your productivity, it's time to follow Gloria Steinem's advice. She said, "Each of us needs a free place, a little psychic territory. This is not a luxury; it's a necessity if we don't want our energy to run dry."

If your energy is running dry or if you're finding it difficult to work on your idea because there's so much competing for your attention, it's time to understand the role ergonomics plays in your ability to get work done and out the door.

Ergonomics is the science of how our environment influences our effectiveness.

A premise of ergonomics is that if you repeatedly do the same type of activity in the same place, you mind automatically associates that activity with that location. For example, if you always open the refrigerator when you walk into the kitchen, you'll find yourself reaching for the refrigerator door as soon as you walk into the kitchen to see if there's anything good to eat. That environment has created a habit, a routine that's become "second nature."

That's why it can be hard to focus on your idea when working at the same desk you use to pay bills and answer emails. Your mind keeps dwelling on the tasks normally associated with that place which makes it difficult to stay focused on the "alien" activity of your creative work. You are fighting your nature – the habitual behavior that is customarily done in that setting.

That's why it's crucial to your creativity to find your Third Place.

What's this about a Third Place? Well, your home is your First Place. Your office is your Second Place. If you work out of a home office, that's both your First and Second Place.

The problem is, your First and Second Place come with built-in associations and distractions. At work, there may be co-workers walking around, customers asking questions, bosses giving orders . . . not to mention ringing phones and click-clacking copiers. At home, you may be thinking about fixing dinner, doing a load of laundry, or keeping an eye on your kids.

That's why one of the best things you can do to become a successful IDEApreneur is to find a different place, a *Third* Place – a public place you can work in private. (And no, that's not an oxymoron.) Your Third Place could be your local Starbucks, library, bookstore, hotel lobby …

anywhere you can take your notepad or laptop and work anonymously and without interruption.

The beauty of your Third Place is that:

- There are no chores to be done, phone calls to return or people to answer to, so you have the freedom to stay focused.
- It becomes your designated place to write, create and think up ideas – it's the only thing you do there – so idea-storming in that location becomes "second nature."
- You create a "cocoon of concentration" and that blissful stream-of-consciousness state of **FLOW** in which your surroundings slip away and you lose yourself in your work.

There's another crucial payoff of repeatedly, exclusively working on your "idea project" in your Third Place. Does the name Pavlov ring a bell? If you go to your Third Place every Saturday morning at 8 to work on your idea, every Saturday morning at 8 to work on your idea; guess what happens the third or fourth time you go?

As soon as you arrive on the premises, your creative faucet opens up and inspiration pours out of your head so fast your fingers will hardly be able to keep up. You will have created a Pavlovian ritual that fast-forwards that exquisite, optimal, peak-performance state of *flow*.

I know you're busy, but surely you can carve out an hour each week to go to your Third Place to focus on your idea project. Doing this ritual will scale your success as an IDEApreneur because you're taking responsibility for consistently moving your project forward – no matter what.

By the way, Ron finished his book "*Is Your Glass Laugh Full?*" because he found his Third Place. A friend who was the General Manager of a nearby Hyatt arranged for him to work in an empty hotel room … proving that it doesn't matter so much *where you work* as long as you *do work* in a ritualistic place that provides the type of idea-friendly ergonomics that support instead of sabotage your efforts to get work done.

Questions to Ask – Actions to Take

1. Do you have a "room of your own" – a Third Place – to incubate your ideas? Describe it.
2. Where can you work, uninterrupted, on your ideas? How can you establish favorable ergonomics – a "creative cocoon of concentration" – so you immerse yourself in your ideas?

CHAPTER 4
Create Real-Life Ideas by Connecting with Real-Life People

"Fear stops most people from writing, not lack of talent. Who am I? What right have I to speak? Who will listen to me? You are a human being with a unique story to tell. You have every right."
– author **Richard Rhodes**

RICHARD RHODES insight applies to IDEApreneurs too. It's not lack of talent, or an absence of ideas, that keep many people from monetizing their mind. It's fear.

I've also discovered, through first-hand experience, that what keeps many of us from monetizing our mind is we become isolated. We lose sight of, or contact with, our intended customers.

When that happens, idea creation becomes an intellectual exercise. Idea-creation isn't supposed to be an *intellectual* exercise; it's supposed to be an empathetic exercise.

Here's what I mean. I love to write. There are many times my mind is on fire and the thoughts are flowing out so fast my fingers can hardly keep up.

It was a surprise, then, while working on my book ***Tongue Fu® at School***, that writing became hard work. I was grinding out pages because I needed to turn my manuscript in to my publisher at the end of the month, but the words just weren't coming.

I would re-read what I had written (I know, a fatal error) and would go "Argghh." The copy was okay, but it didn't sing, it wasn't "alive."

I was creatively procrastinating one morning (reading the newspaper instead of working on the book) when I came across a fascinating article in *USA Today* about David Kelly, at that time, one of Hollywood's "Golden Boys."

The article pointed out that, for a while, writer/director Kelly could do no wrong. He was the first person to receive an Emmy for Best Comedy *(Ally McBeal)* and Best Drama *(The Practice)* the same year. Incredibly, Kelly was writing and directing *both* shows at the same time.

Then, for some reason, things started going south. Kelly's new pilot didn't get picked up. His shows were dropping in the ratings. The reporter thought it was because his plots were becoming rather bizarre. Mainstream viewers were having a hard time relating to his unrealistic story lines.

When asked why Kelly had lost the golden touch, a TV critic postulated it was because he had lost the common touch. "He lives in a $15-million-dollar home, he's married to Michelle Pfeiffer and all he does is write, drive to the studio, direct, drive home, repeat. He's disconnected."

A light bulb went off in my head. Here I was trying to write a book about dealing with difficult people in schools – and I wasn't spending any time talking with people in schools. I had lost the "common touch." **Writing had become an intellectual exercise**. I was trying to figure out what to say in my disassociated mind instead of connecting with my target readers and asking what they thought, wanted and needed - what they were dealing with on a daily basis.

I got up from my chair and drove to my sons' high school. That day I interviewed several teachers, the principal, a guidance counselor, and several of my sons' friends.

I asked teachers, "What do you do when a parent accuses you of not caring for their kid or when kids don't turn in their homework on time?" I asked the principal, "What do you when teachers complain they're not getting paid enough (which is true)?" I asked students, "What do you do when a classmate bullies you or when someone's bothering you on the bus?"

After a few hours of listening to them pour out their frustrations, my mind was filled with the insights, anger, concerns, success stories, challenges, mini-victories and mixed feelings of pride and powerlessness that is a fact of life for many educators, school counselors and students.

I sat down to the computer as soon as I got home and the real-life situations I had heard were integrated into the book and made it sing. One afternoon of re-connecting with my intended audience renewed my passion for my project and brought the words alive – because I had gotten out of my head and into the real world of my target readers.

Has your creative project come to a screeching halt? For some reason, have the ideas dried up?

Perhaps this project has become an intellectual exercise. Perhaps you're grinding it out because you've got a deadline and you've become completely detached from your intended audience and purpose. Perhaps you've become distant and removed from your target customers.

That doesn't work because that's one-sided communication. That's simply purging what's in your head. You're trying to produce ideas – in a vacuum. If your intent is simply to finish, you can accomplish that – but that won't make it sing. You will have a completed project, but it will be lifeless and working on it will be joyless.

For creative work to become transcendent, we must have a clear idea of how it will deliver value for people. We need to visualize specific (or connect with) individuals in our target audience and imagine how this project, product or program will solve problems they're currently facing.

When we develop our idea with specific target individuals in mind, when we're envisioning how they will benefit from this, our heartfelt intention to bridge the gap that exists between us creates a connection that can be felt even if we never meet in person.

This is what happened to couple of colleagues. Woody and Eleanor Rupp, long-time high school teachers, were working on a book in which they shared what students had told them they wished their parents knew. We came up with a great title for their book that every parent instantly gets … *Long Days, Short Years.*

They had a tight deadline, but were offered an opportunity to speak on a cruise. They told me they were probably going to turn down the cruise because they needed to finish their book.

I said, "Want some unsolicited input?" and they said, "Sure."

"GO ON THE CRUISE," I told them. **Crowd-sourcing is not taking time away from *your* book**; it's the best investment you can make in your book. You can interview all the parents and grandparents. While walking around the ship, playing bridge, or sharing dinner, you can ask people, "What's something you did as a parent that worked out well? What's something you regret or that backfired despite your best intentions? What's one piece of advice you'd give to parents with young children?" You'll be crowd-sourcing your content. Your book will be better because it will contain a recent, more diverse offering of insights and lessons-learned.

Suffice it to say, Eleanor and Woody went on that cruise. Not only did they have a marvelous time; they were the toast of the ship. Not only did they meet their deadline, they were able to fill their book with insightful RUPdates that added real-world value for readers.

Are you wondering, "Good for them, but what's this got to do with becoming an IDEApreneur?"

Please know that *people love being asked for their advice.* Malcolm Forbes said, "The way to a man's heart is through his opinion." The way to almost anyone's heart is through their advice.

Crowd-sourcing your content by interviewing individuals in your target market is beneficial for you (you get to feed off their energy instead of supplying all your own) and it ensures your ideas are being developed in organic alignment with your customers' current needs and interests.

A participant in one of my strategic retreats said, "Sam, what if we don't have the luxury of leaving our office to connect with customers? I don't think my boss would like it too much if I walked out of work every afternoon to go interview people."

There's another way to interview your target audience – without getting up from your chair.

I had the good fortune to interview prolific *New York Times* best-selling author James Rollins. James' thriller *Map of Bones* was chosen by Publishers Weekly as the book "most likely to win over Dan Brown's (*The DaVinci Code*) faithful audience."

I was curious as to how and why James has been able to produce so many bestsellers in such a short time (ten in less than eight years) and asked him, "Where do you get your ideas?"

James said, "After writing a dozen books, you can't rely on the 'hand of God' to tap you on the shoulder and deliver an inspired idea for a book. So, I subscribe to a lot of magazines ranging from *Discover* to *Scientific American* – anything to do with my interests which are animals, physics, inventions.

I also read a lot of newspapers every day, looking for some interesting tidbit that makes it through my screen. If it catches my interest, it means it's new instead of being commonplace which means it has potential to be explored. Keeping my antennae up for these types of 'didn't know that' ideas turns writing into a never-ending adventure for me and my readers."

Great insight, James. I agree with him about the power of scrolling Facebook, subscribing to TED talks, and reading related publications to trigger new ideas. Just as a jazz pianist riffs off standard chords to create new music, we can riff off what we read and watch to create new ideas.

Please notice I said "riff off," not "rip off." Always, always attribute the source of your ideas. Give credit where credit is due.

I love reading the weekend editions of *Wall Street Journal*, *New York Times* and *Washington Post*. I never read one of these fascinating publications without finding at least two or three intriguing articles or quotes that pique my curiosity and that would add value for my program participants, consulting clients, or blog readers.

And no, I don't read the news. My goal is not to become depressed by man's inhumanity to man. My goal is to become enlightened or inspired by man's humanity to man – so I read interviews and features of business leaders, pop culture icons, athletes, successful entertainers and entrepreneurs to discover their back-stories, best practices and lessons-learned.

You feed your body with nourishing meals. Why not feed your brain with nourishing material? To get maximum value from your reading, don't read randomly – read with a purpose. Prime your mental pump with questions that screen out the irrelevant and search for pertinent insights your intended audience will find interesting and useful such as:

- What recent research has surprising findings that would add to their knowledge?
- What would stop them in their mental tracks because it's controversial, counter-intuitive, or flies in the face of what they currently believe?
- What organizations are in the news due to their remarkable success in your field? What breakthroughs or leading-edge trends are happening in your profession?
- What revolutionary new products, services, approaches are disrupting the norm?

When you come across tidbits that cause your eyebrows to go up, (a sure sign of curiosity), realize they will probably get your target audiences' eyebrows up too. Like James Rollins said, these ideas have broken through your filter and piqued your curiosity – they'll probably pique the curiosity of your intended customers.

Questions to Ask – Actions to Take

1. Have you lost touch with your target customers? Are you operating in isolation and idea creation has become an intellectual exercise? Explain.
2. How are you going to crowd-source your topic, idea or invention by asking "real-life" people what they think, want, feel, need? How will you turn your idea-creation into an empathetic exercise by accessing individuals who could benefit from what you're offering, who might want to try/buy or fund it, and could become word-of-mouth ambassadors for it who take it viral?

CHAPTER 5
Where Do You Get Your Ideas?

*"Have I stretched the envelope as much as I want? No.
That's why I'm still creatively hungry."*
– Stephen Spielberg

DID YOU SEE Academy-award winning movie *Little Miss Sunshine*?

Its screenwriter, Michael Arndt, suffered through years of trying to get it produced … to no avail. In fact, he worked as an assistant to Matthew Broderick (*Ferris Bueller's Day Off*) so he could stay involved in the movie industry and meet potential investors and directors who might support his creative projects.

During the Q and A following Michael's keynote for our Maui Writers Conference, a participant asked, "How did you get the idea for your screenplay?"

He said, "I was watching TV coverage of the Jon Benet Ramsey trial and they played a video clip of a beauty pageant for young girls. I watched the elaborately coiffed 'Stepford dolls' mince across the stage and thought, "Wouldn't it be cool if a plain, plump girl entered the contest and rocked the house?"

That was the genesis of his break-out film about a spunky, pudgy girl (the fantastic Abigail Breslin) and her dysfunctional family driving cross country to a beauty pageant.

When another audience member asked, "Where did you get the idea for the malfunctioning VW bus?" Michael said, "Well, our family went on vacation one summer, and the clutch in our VW bus …" The audience erupted in laughter. (If you saw this very funny movie, you know why.)

The point? **When something captures your attention, pay attention.** It means this idea broke through your mind's screen – which is hard to do. Of the thousands of images and items your mind notices every day, this particular idea was sufficiently interesting to "come" to your attention. That means it has the potential to become an Equity Idea.

Michael Arndt didn't watch that beauty pageant passively; he watched it proactively. He asked himself those two idea-inspiring words, "What if …"

Those two words "What if …" are the origin of innovation.

Look around you right now. Instead of just accepting "what is" ask yourself "What if … ?"

- What if we did that a different way?
- What if I sped this up, slowed this down, turned it upside down?
- What if I made it bigger, smaller, fancier, simpler?
- What if I altered this to make it more timely, current or convenient?
- What if I did the opposite of the always?

Rossbeth Moss Kanter said, "Creativity is like looking at the world through a kaleidoscope.

You look at a set of elements, the same ones everyone else sees, but then reassemble those floating bits and pieces into an enticing new possibility."

IDEApreneur

My favorite example of a company that re-arranged the kaleidoscope is Heinz catsup. How long have people been pounding their palms on the bottom of a ketchup bottle in a labor-intensive (and frustrating) effort to get that slow-moving condiment out?

I'm guessing someone on the creative team at Heinz had a "Duh" moment. As in, "Duh, what if we turned the bottle upside down and let gravity work for us instead of against us?"

With that simple innovation, their catsup bottle now rests on its cap. All people have to do is open the cap and the catsup is right there, waiting to be squirted out. Voila.

Curved shower rods is another "duh" invention. For decades, people complained about cramped tubs or crowded shower stalls in hotels.

Finally, someone thought, "Hmm, we don't have to go to the considerable expense of enlarging the bathroom, tub or shower stall. We can give people more space simply by curving the shower rod out so people have more space to move around."

What a simple solution to a problem affecting millions of people … for a fraction of the cost of tearing out walls and enlarging the tub, or installing a new shower stall.

Think about it. We can put men and women in space, communicate instantly with people on the other side of the world, drive anywhere without getting lost thanks to our GPS systems – but it took decades to solve these recurring, relatively simple to solve, problems.

The point I'm making? There are "duh" inventions and innovations all around us just waiting for someone to think of a better, easier, faster, cheaper, safer way to live life and do business.

You could be that someone. How does your idea turn a "What is" into a "What if?" How can you re-arrange the kaleidoscope in your profession, field or industry to come up with that better way?

Saddled with an "embarrassing" identifier, the Sioux City, Iowa airport considered asking the FAA if they could change it. Then, their airport director thought, "Wait a minute. What if, instead of being embarrassed by our name SUX, we capitalized on it?"

In a bold move, they decided to turn their embarrassment into an advantage. Their new marketing campaign *FlyingSUX* and its associated line of *FlySUX* t-shirts and caps have gone viral and become so popular, airlines have *added* flights to the airport. "Now the whole world knows about us," airport Director Rick McElroy says, "in a positive way."

Think about the enormity of what they did. **They turned an existing problem that was *costing* them money into a competitive edge that is *making* them money. Proof that creative ideas, positioning and messaging aren't petty; they're profitable.**

Creativity means not being content to be common. You don't want to follow the crowd.

You don't even want to lead the crowd. You want to create your own crowd.

Want one more example of the power of adopting a "What if?" mentality? Victoria Colligan and Beth Schoenfeldt, successful New York sales/marketing professionals, were discussing an unflattering perception of New York women as "Ladies who lunch." They wondered, "What if, instead of meeting to discussing shopping, charity balls or trendy restaurants, women met to strategize their business ventures?" The result? **Ladies Who Launch**, a nationwide organization that supports women entrepreneurs in incubating successful businesses.

As artist Jasper Johns said, "Take an object. Do something to it. Do something *else* to it."

Look beyond the surface of what's around you. Turn "What is" into "What if?" Experiment with the resulting variations until you create something that didn't exist before. If you want to create Equity Ideas, don't be satisfied to simply *stretch* the envelope; create a *brand new* envelope.

Want more examples of companies that have created Equity Ideas? Check out my book *Got Your Attention?* I share the back-story of Uber and Snuba – both revolutionary ideas that disrupted an existing category and created entirely new categories that have generated millions in profits.

Questions to Ask – Actions to Take

1. What are a couple of your favorite "duh" discoveries? Like the curved shower rod, catsup bottles that sit on their head, or UBER which disrupted a taxi industry that had operated the same way for decades … what are ideas and inventions that introduced a new, better way?
2. Look at the problem you want to solve. A need you want to fill. A business you want to build. Ask yourself, "What is … ?" What is the norm, the SOP (standard operating procedure)?
3. Now, ask yourself, "What if … ?" What if we did it a different way, faster, easier, less expensive way? Keep doing something else to that norm until you create something new.

CHAPTER 6
Attain, Sustain and Regain the IDEA Zone

"You can't think and swing at the same time."
*– **Yogi Berra** to baseball player*

HAVE YOU EXPERIENCED this exquisite state of flow athletes refer to as the "zone?"

Perhaps, like Masters champion Jordan Spieth, you had a round of golf in which you were playing "out of your head" and played better than you knew how. Perhaps you were playing tennis and placing your serves and shots exactly where you wanted. Or, maybe you were skiing in fresh powder and completely, joyfully focused on whooshing down the slope. Bliss, wasn't it?

A participant in a workshop said, "Sam, I don't play sports but I get in the zone when I'm gardening." She's right. We can access this focused state of "entrainment" when gardening on a spring day, playing a guitar or the piano, or reading a novel by our favorite author.

Entrainment is when you're so swept up in what you're doing; you're one with it. When you're immersed in this state of flow, you're totally absorbed, not even aware of your surroundings or the passage of time. Ironically, when you lose yourself in your work, you do your best work. In my book *ConZentrate*, (which *7 Habits of Highly Effective People* author Stephen Covey endorsed as "thought-provoking, fascinating"), I share dozens of innovative ways to achieve a peak performance state that improves your *work and athletic* flow.

This chapter explains how to achieve **Creative ConZONEtration** to improve your idea flow.

First, it's important to understand you can *facilitate* flow, you can't *force* it. In fact, the harder you "try" to concentrate, the more it will elude you.

The good news is, there are specific ways to increase the likelihood flow will show.

The first is to avoid the one thing that kills Creative Concentration … *self*-consciousness.

Athletes, artists, entrepreneurs all agree that the peak performance state of flow is a *stream*-of-conscious state. You're simply doing whatever it is you're *doing*; you're not *thinking* about it.

You're simply playing the music as beautifully as you know how; you're not thinking about which finger is on what key. You're simply skiing down the hill, not thinking about the hot tub waiting for you at the lodge. You're dialed in and hitting your golf ball straight down the fairway and straight at the flag, not thinking about club swing, knees, wrists, elbows and torque. You're reveling in digging in the dirt, not thinking about emails you need to answer.

In a weird way, the second you become aware you're in a state of flow, it's gone. The second you second-guess this state, ("I can't believe I'm playing par golf. I've never broken 100 before" or "I can't believe I'm pitching a perfect game") it is gone.

Self-consciousness is the antithesis of *stream*-of-consciousness.

What does that mean for you when you're trying to kick-start your creativity and generate ideas?

IDEApreneur

The key to getting in the flow of thinks (pun intended) is to establish a mental momentum in which your ideas are flowing freely *without fear or judgement.*

To achieve Creative ConZONEtration, promise yourself you won't second-guess ideas as they occur to you. The instant you start questioning the feasibility of a fresh idea, any other fragile ideas queuing up to come out will say, "Uh-uh. I'm not going out there. Forget about it."

Bestselling author Jacquelyn Mitchard, Oprah's first Book Club pick for *The Deep End of the Ocean*, learned the consequences of second-guessing self-criticism the hard way.

I asked Jackie how she managed to write all her books from home while raising seven children.

Jackie explained that when her first husband died, she found herself supporting her family with her writing. "I couldn't afford to dawdle over my manuscripts anymore because my ability to pay bills depended on my advances and royalties. **I used to re-read what I had written the day before. But then I'd end up re-writing what I had written. At the end of the week, I'd have the same 10-20 pages and they weren't necessarily better, they were just ... different.**

"I consciously decided to stop correcting as I go. Now I review the last page from the previous day and write forward from there. I finish books in a fraction of the time it used to take. I make progress every day instead of re-working things to death and taking the voice out of them."

Smart woman. One reason Jackie has developed such a lucrative, respected career as an author and journalist is because she stopped second-guessing herself, started trusting her instincts and focused on producing, producing, producing ... which results in mental momentum and flow.

Stop Second-Guessing Yourself

"In order to get in touch I have to block out ego. Ego is the piece of me that's going, 'How am I doing, champ?' That has nothing to do with creating. That has to do with the finished work and that's a separate creature. I need to work from within, not critiquing, not judging, but being still enough to hear the voice that'll tell me what I'm supposed to do next." – author Sue Grafton

As the saying goes, "Draft, then craft. First get it written, then get it right."

I have had the privilege of working with a lot of entrepreneurs to build their brands and businesses. EO (Entrepreneurs Organization) has hired me to speak for them around the world, at events in Athens, London, Geneva, Berlin, Toronto, Vancouver, Chicago, New York, St. Moritz, Portland, Los Angeles, Denver, Austin, Houston, Boston, and Phoenix.

Our goal is to come up with a one-of-a-kind equity brand that gives them a competitive edge so they stand out in their marketplace and scale their profits. When strategizing potential names, domains, titles and taglines, I've developed a verbal tic that keeps the self-conscious critic at bay.

I don't know *when* I started doing this, but I know *why*.

When brainstorming the perfect title, brand or positioning statement, it's vital for us both to feel comfortable being un-perfect (if that's not a word, it should be.)

If we're tossing out ideas and something occurs to me that seems a little "out there," the words ***"Just playing"*** pop out of my mouth. That phrase frees me to blurt out what's on my mind ... without premature evaluation.

A client looked at me with a puzzled expression one time and said, "Sam, that's the fourth time you've said that. Why do you keep saying, 'Just playing?'"

It was then I realized this had become a verbal tic – albeit a good one. It's my way of giving my brain permission to come out and play. It's my way of feeling comfortable voicing something that may initially seem off-brand, unfeasible or irrelevant.

I've come to understand, "**To connect new dots, we must feel comfortable voicing new thoughts.**"

And new thoughts almost always seem "out there." Unrealistic. Impossible. Random.

If you want to come up with a new idea, something no one else has already done, vow to voice "dots and thoughts" that don't make sense. Remind yourself, if the idea makes sense, someone else has probably already done it.

If you pre-judge an idea's potential, you'll stifle your creativity. If you consistently shut down new ideas, the creative source feels chastised and closes up shop. Instead, adopt your own verbal version of "Just playing," so your mind feels free to voice "out there" dots and thoughts that, when connected, yield an innovative approach that advances the field.

Give Random Thoughts a Chance

Remember John Lennon's song "Give Peace a Chance?"

When you give "random thoughts" a chance, they may surprise you by leading to an even BETTER idea that wouldn't have happened if that first idea had been cut off at the knees.

I've learned this from first-hand experience. Often, during a consult, a client will start talking passionately about something that seems to be "off agenda." They'll catch themselves and apologize, saying, "Sorry to get us off track."

I laugh and say, "**That wasn't off track, that was top of mind**. We're going to write it down, because it's going in the mix. You feel strongly about this which means it's important. It wanted to be said. We may not understand how, where or why yet ... but that is going to play a role in us coming up with a brand, business or book that stands out and makes your heart sing."

Invariably, later that weekend or on our next consult, the lights will go on and the band will play and we'll suddenly see how that "dot and thought" led to creating something unique and viable.

So, ask yourself, "Do I have perfectionist tendencies? Am I my own worst critic? Do I prejudge an idea's feasibility and let doubts get the best of me?"

Please re-read the above sentence. "Get the best of me." You'll never be able to do your best work if you continue to second-guess your originality.

Next time you're tempted to judge your "dots and thoughts," read Leonard Bernstein's quote below to remind yourself to "let it flow, let it flow, let it *flow*."

"You can sit there, tense and worried, freezing the creative energies or you can start writing something, perhaps something silly. It simply doesn't matter what. In five or ten minutes, the imagination will heat, the tightness will fade and a certain spirit and rhythm will take over."

Isn't that eloquent? If you want your imagination to heat, tell that critic to get lost. Generate ideas, don't judge them. Unfreeze your creative energies by producing, producing, producing. Come back when you're finished to fine-tune. Draft, then craft. Get it written, then get it right.

In the years that I've studied this topic and developed this system for becoming an entrepreneur, I've come up with specific ways to Attain, Sustain and Regain the all-important IDEA Zone.

Intrigued? Keep reading …

Attain a Flow of Ideas

"I have walked myself into my best thoughts."
– Soren Kierkegaard

WALKING is my idea factory. What's yours?

Walking – getting a move on – is one of the most enjoyable ways to facilitate the flow of ideas.

This is not petty; it's pivotal.

Think about it. Ideas don't happen in inertia. If we're sedentary, our mind will be sedentary. If we want to activate our imagination, we need to activate ourselves.

Movement and flow are inextricably connected. They're like the chicken and the egg. If we want to set up a flow of ideas, we need to set up a flow of movement. One way to do this is by giving ourselves a mental assignment and then going for a swim, run, bike ride or aerobic workout.

Getting our legs and arms moving in a left-right aligned rhythm oxygenates and activates our right and left brain. I know this from experience. I had the privilege of working with Rod Laver (who won the Grand Slam of Tennis twice – an unprecedented accomplishment).

Rocket told me the best way to warm up (mentally and physically) was to stand close to the net and fire volleys back and forth. Why? When you're rat-tat-tatting the ball back and forth so fast … you don't have time to think.

That's the point. You're expediting that un-self-conscious zone state in which you're doing it, not thinking about it.

Baseball players do the same thing by playing catch. Throwing the ball back and forth sets up that sub-conscious state where they're doing it on auto-pilot, without thought. Gymnasts and skaters repeatedly walk through their routine while awaiting their turn in the wings so they stay focused on their upcoming performance instead of their fears. Football field kickers practice their step, step, step, BOOM on the sidelines before an important kick to get themselves into the rhythm of their performance so they can execute it just like they practiced.

What's the point? If you're feeling sluggish, your chance of coming up with any good ideas is slim. If you're mentally burned out, tackling your creative project right now may be a waste of time. The harder you "try," the more frustrated and blocked you'll become. Instead, take a break and go do something else.

Activity is an idea catalyst. You're not avoiding work; you're energizing your work. This "Don't think, do" approach can help you get "unstuck." That's what happened when I was writing **What's Holding You Back? 30 Days to Going Where You Want, Meeting Whom You Want, and Doing What You Want.**

I had a week to turn my book into my St. Martin's Press editor Jennifer Enderlin (who's a delight) and still hadn't finished the Introduction. Not for a lack of trying, mind you. But the harder I tried, the more the right words eluded me.

IDEApreneur

Luckily for me, a confluence of events kick-started the ideal intro. Actually, I call this a conFLOWence of events because when this happens it's like the jigsaw puzzle pieces of your idea are falling into place. It's sublime.

I was in Denver, Colorado for a speaking engagement and was staying with my friend Mary Loverde (author of *The Invitation* and *Stop Screaming at the Microwave*). After a delightful breakfast in her sunny kitchen, we headed to the gym to work out.

I jumped on the treadmill (strategically placed in front of floor-to-ceiling windows with a sweeping view of the majestic Rockies) and started walking briskly, thinking about my book. In minutes, the Intro "came" to me. I jumped off the treadmill, borrowed some paper and one of those scrubby little pencils, sat on one of those narrow benches in the locker room and scribbled down the thoughts pouring out of my mind as fast as I could. It came out perfect. I wouldn't change a word. In fact, when I turned in the manuscript, Jen phoned me with one of the most magnificent compliments I've ever received. She said, "Sam, it flows like a symphony. I wouldn't change a word."

I'm convinced the main reason that Intro "flowed like a symphony" was because I stopped trying to "think it up" - an intellectual exercise which is the opposite of the stream-of-conscious state of creativity. The physical activity jump-started my Idea Zone.

A woman in one of my POP! presentations put her hand up and said, "You forgot one of the best ways to achieve the Idea Zone."
Surprised, I asked, "What's that?"

She said, "Get a dog."

The audience laughed and she explained, "I have a home-based business selling vintage clothing on eBay. I know it's important to exercise, but I'm a sole proprietor. There's so much to do and nobody to do it but me, so it's easy to get caught up and work straight through the day. Sometimes I get so busy, I don't even go to the bathroom."

"A few months ago, my best friend moved to an apartment complex that doesn't allow pets. That meant she couldn't take her Border Collie with her, so I agreed to take him. Buddy the Border Collie has so much energy I've got to walk him several times a day. After a few hours go by with me being glued to the computer processing orders, he'll come over, put his paw on my arm and look at me with those bright hopeful eyes as if to say, 'Come on outside, the graphics are great.'"

"I do my best thinking on those walks. I always give my mind an assignment – how to streamline my operation, describe clothes more enticingly, reduce packaging costs, something. I always – and I mean always - come up with a better way to run my business on those walks. That dog is responsible for a lot of money-making ideas."

Another woman put her hand up (and I'll always be glad she did) and offered a counterpoint to this suggestion. She said, "Moving is not so easy for me. I have arthritis and joint pain. I can't just jump up and go for a walk around the block. You know what I do when I want to solve a problem or make progress on a project?"

Everyone in the class looked at her, waiting for her response.

She said, with a twinkle in her eye, "I take a shower. THAT'S what gets the *stream* of consciousness going for me."

Another woman laughed and said, "Guess what I do? I wash the dishes. Our kitchen sink looks out over a field. I love rinsing and washing the dishes while gazing out at nature. The water flowing over my hands puts me in a kind of reverie, almost a meditative Zen state."

Excellent points. There are a lot of ways to facilitate flow. The bottom-line is, *do* whatever works for you. Getting your *body* in motion can get your *brain* in motion. Being in or around the flow of water – whether in a shower or washing the dishes – can free up mental gridlock. Whatever you do, if the ideas aren't coming … don't think, do.

Sustain a Flow of Ideas

YEARS AGO, some friends and I were playing golf one beautiful summer afternoon and discussing Tiger Woods' uncanny ability to out-perform other world-class golfers.

Things have changed for Tiger since his highly public divorce and physical injuries, however he was in a class by himself for more than a decade. We agreed that a major contributor to his impressive string of wins in international tournaments was his almost super-human ability to sustain his focus while his opponents were losing theirs.

Tiger was renowned for his powers of concentration. This didn't happen by chance. His dad (who started teaching Tiger when he was just 3 years old) taught Tiger how to stay in flow – no matter what – by deliberately jangling a can of coins when he was trying to putt. Or, he would shout out a question just as Tiger was drawing his club back to tee off. Tiger's father wasn't being mean – he just knew how crucial it was for Tiger to get accustomed to distractions so he could ignore them when playing in pressure-packed PGA tournaments.

If you've watched Tiger compete, you may have noticed his distinctive ritual to help him block out his surroundings. He cups his hands around his eyes –like putting blinkers on a horse – to shut out the noisy gallery, TV cameras and scoreboard so they are "out of sight, out of mind."

How does using your hands as "blinkers" help you stay focused? **Imagine your mind as a camera and your eyes as the aperture. Understand that** *our attention is where our eyes are.*

Most of the time, our eyes are sweeping our surroundings which means we're registering everything we're seeing which means we're thinking many things at once.

We actually can operate pretty well in this wide-angle lens mode. You've probably had the experience of working at your desk, listening to Pandora, checking email and thinking about a meeting that's in ten minutes. You may have been preparing dinner while watching news AND thinking about the dish in the microwave AND calling the kids to come to the table.

This wide-angle lens thinking works fine most of the time.

But it is NOT conducive to the idea zone. You've heard of multi-tasking? Well, this is like multi-thinking. Multi-thinking compromises Creative ConZONEtration because you're not focusing exclusively on your idea. It precludes you from getting in your IDEA Zone.

If you want to attain and maintain Creative ConZONEtration, you need to learn how to switch to and stay in telephoto focus.

The way to do that is to use a version of Tiger's trick. You can try this right now. Place your hands around your eyes to block out your surroundings so they are "out of sight, out of mind." Gaze at something specific (a painting on a nearby wall, a photo on your desk.) Continue to keep your hands cupped around your eyes and look solely at that object. You will find you're no longer thinking about other things because you are narrowing your field of vision and giving your *undivided* attention to your selected priority.

Using your hands as blinkers is doubly effective because, if you do it every single time you want to pay attention to your idea, this act becomes a Pavlovian ritual that cues your ConZONEtration.

IDEApreneur

Remember Pavlov? Ring the bell, feed the dog. Ring the bell, feed the dog. After a while you just have to ring the bell and the dog salivates. If you use your hands as blinkers every time you want to switch from multi-thinking to single-thinking … it will only be a matter of time before, the moment you put your hands around your eyes, you automatically shut out your surroundings and concentrate completely on what's in sight, in mind.

A woman in a *You Can Concentrate* workshop asked, "Sam, isn't this a little like your suggestion to work in our Third Place so writing in that space becomes a ritual?"

Exactly. In fact, one of my consulting clients said she combined these two Pavlovian rituals to finish her book.

Bev said, "I have a little coffee shop around the corner from my office that's a favorite hangout. Writing at home doesn't work for me because of my family and writing at work is a nono – so the only free time I have is lunch. After our first session, I decided to go there two days a week until I finished my book. I got a table in back and tried to write but found myself looking up all the time and checking out the people walking by.

"Then I remembered Tiger's technique. I turned my chair around so I was facing the back of the coffee shop. I cupped my hands around my eyes and told myself that for the next 45 minutes, I was going to give my complete, undivided attention to producing two pages. After a few times, the very act of putting on my "blinkers" helps me get down to business. It really does work."

Want another way to help yourself sustain flow and focus in a distracting environment? Get rid of those U.P.O.'s. *What* are U.P.O.'s? Unidentified Piled Objects.

Imagine you're at your computer. On your desk sits a stack of letters you need to answer, along with ten phone messages you need to return and an in-basket with bills you need to pay. Every time your eyes move just a few inches away from your screen, you're thinking about everything BUT your priority project. "Ohmigosh, I was supposed to call Bill yesterday. When am I going to have time to answer those letters? Those invoices should have gone out yesterday."

What does this mean? As long as you have a cluttered workspace with U.P.O.'s, you'll constantly interrupt your train of thought – making it almost impossible to attain or sustain the desired state of Creative ConZONEtration.

What to do? **Nurture your creative nature by immersing yourself in nature**. Gazing at nature is like going to a mind spa. It's like giving your brain a little massage, a little spiritual respite.

This is another of those ideas that may sound trivial; however, it's vital. I'm fortunate. For the past decade, I've lived on a lake. My desk faces floor-to-ceiling windows that overlook water. When I'm searching for just the right words, I look out the window and let my mind wander while my eyes rest on the water, trees, sky and greenery. Looking at nature – which is dynamic and full of vitality even when it is still – fuels idea generation. More often than not, the right thought occurs to me and I'm off and running (well, off and writing).

A program participant said, "Sam, that must be nice, but I work in an office that doesn't have any windows." Another chimed in with, "My desk is next to a window but it looks out at a brick building across the street." Another asked, "What about those of us who work in cubicles?"

Turn your cubicle into a "view-bicle." If you don't have a work space that looks out at nature, bring nature into your work space. Clear the clutter off your desk (so it's out of sight, out of mind) and replace it with a vase with a single beautiful flower.

Why a single flower, not a bouquet? An assortment of flowers has too many aspects to look at and think about. Your eyes would flit from one bud or one leaf to another and you'd end up comparing them and assessing them.

The goal isn't to think about the flowers, the goal is to let your eyes and mind rest on a flower so you can absorb and immerse yourself in its beauty while staying deep in thought. The goal is to give yourself a visual and mental break without losing your train of thought.

When you gaze at a single flower, you soak in its natural beauty without moving your eyes (or mind). Your mind is nourished but not distracted. Your temporarily tired mind gets to mull for a while – and you go back to work a moment later, refreshed and replenished. This may sound "woo-woo," but it works.

The last year my sons and I lived in Hawaii, we lived in a home that didn't have a nice view of nature. Heck, it didn't have any view of nature. The only windows we had looked out at streets or our neighbor's houses over our side and backyard fence. Hardly inspiring stuff.

The good news was, this house had at least ten rose bushes in constant bloom (love that year-round 70-80 degree sunshine!) My morning ritual was to walk Tom and Andrew to the bus stop, and then come back and snip one rose each morning and put it on my desk next to my computer.

Whenever my mind temporarily stalled, I would gaze at the rose and muse. Invariably the next idea would come to mind (love that phrase) and I'd return to work, raring to write. If I had looked at my To-Do list instead of that rose, I would have lost my train of thought and who knows if or when I would have gotten back on track?

Try it. In fact, turn this into a weekly ritual to catalyze your Creative ConZONEtration. Every grocery market has a flower section. Or if you live in a large city, there are flower vendors on major street corners. For a couple dollars, you can select a fresh flower every Monday on the way to work. What an inexpensive, yet potentially rewarding indulgence. This week a sunflower. Next week a peony. The following week a cymbidium orchid. Small pleasures. Big results.

From now on, keep your work obligations within reach (a desk drawer?) but not where your eyes will fall on them every other minute and cause you to become preoccupied. Place your fresh flower – a thing of beauty with no associations of obligations that haven't been done– in sight. When you need to take a little mental break, steep your mind's eye in its loveliness and see if it doesn't help you maintain that highly productive state of ConZonetration.

What are you going to do today to give yourself a workspace that is conducive to attaining and maintaining the Idea Zone? Are you going to replace distracting UPO's with a single rose so when your eyes wander your mind doesn't wander too? Are you going to move your desk so it looks out at a window which looks out at nature?

Regain a Flow of Ideas

"Opportunity knocks. People barge right in."
– oh-so-true office poster

A CONSULTING CLIENT asked me, "Okay, I know how to set up and sustain the flow of ideas – but how can I regain my concentration once I lose it? I can be humming along and then Fed Ex makes a delivery and I've got to get up and sign for it, and by the time I come back to my project, I'm mentally dead in the water. I just sit there, staring at the page with my mind blank. Any suggestions?"

Yup. Follow best-selling author Frank McCourt's example. Frank, who won the Pulitzer Prize for *Angela's Ashes*, was a presenter at Maui Writers Conference.

As Emcee, I always went for a walk early in the morning to prepare my introductions and get mentally organized so I could keep the conference running smoothly and professionally.

One morning, as I was walking along the beach path that runs in front of our host hotel, I saw Frank, sitting by himself, writing. He was doing something puzzling that caught my attention. He'd write in one notebook, pause, look up, scribble something in his other notebook and then resume writing in the first. As I got closer, I could see his notebooks were the kind with the black squiggles on the cover you use for high-school tests. (You may know Frank was a high school English teacher for many years.)

Normally, I wouldn't disturb a writer's reverie, however I was curious and thought I'd ask a quick question and be on my way. I greeted Frank, apologized for interrupting, promised to be brief and told him, "I can't help but wonder … why the two notebooks?"

Frank smiled and explained, "I always write first thing in the morning to capture that dreamlike state you have when you first wake up. I found though that I'd be making progress on my novel and then think of something mundane like 'Don't forget to pick up the dry cleaning.' Before you know it, I would have lost my train of thought and couldn't get it back. I started bringing another notebook with me and when a 'to do' occurs to me, I write it down in my other notebook so (and then he said something really profound) … I'm free to forget it."

Think about Frank's powerful words. Free to forget it.

If we're lucky enough to achieve that lovely state of "mental momentum" and then we remember something else we need to do, our goal is to handle that disruption in a way that makes it a temporary rather than permanent distraction.

If you make a written note of that task (whether it's to buy a birthday card or return a phone call), we no longer have to keep it top of mind where it's splitting our focus. Our mind no longer has to serve as a bulletin board with all these little yellow mental "post-its." We can return to our creative project, content that our written reminders will be there waiting for us when we're finished and it's time to attend to them.

Want to know another way to regain creative concentration following an interruption? BEFORE you drop what you're doing to sign for the package from the Fed Ex man or whatever . . .simply ask yourself, "What was I going to say next?"

Take a second to write down a key word of what you were going to say next before you abandon your creative project and switch your attention to something else.

If you do this, a magical thing happens. When you come back to your original project, instead of staring at the page in frustration and going "ARGGH, I can't remember where I was going with this," your train of thought is right there waiting for you on the page. All you have to do is look at that key word and you'll hit the mental ground running.

Prolific author Isaac Asimov (more than 100 books!) was asked the secret to his writing output. He said, "Nothing interferes with my concentration. You could put on an orgy in my office and I wouldn't look up. Well, maybe once."

Next time you're "in the zone" and something pulls you away, simply ask yourself, "Where was I going with this?" Jot that thought so you can give your full attention to whoever or whatever needs your attention for that moment – content that when you return, all you have to do is glance at your trigger word and you'll be back in that lovely state of Creative ConZONEtration.

Questions to Ask – Actions to Take

1. How will you prevent the type of self-consciousness that blocks Creative ConZONEtration?
2. What are you going to tell yourself when something occurs to you that at first seems impractical, unreasonable or unworkable? What is your verbal version of "Just playing?"
3. How will you keep your second-guessing critic at bay? How will you be sure to capture new "dots and thoughts" so they can go into the mix to create something unique and original?
4. How will you attain and maintain the flow of ideas by getting a move on? By using "blinkers" around your eyes to block-out surroundings so they're out of sight, out of mind?
5. How will you regain the flow of ideas by jotting down distracting thoughts so you're free to forget them? How will you set up a Pavlovian ritual to concentrate on command so you can kick-start your creativity and expedite your IDEA zone?

SECTION II
Complete Your W-5 Form So Your Ideas Are Commercially Viable

"Great ideas need landing gears as well as wings."
– Coffee Mug slogan

ONCE WE KNOW how to increase our flow of ideas, we need to learn how to make sure those ideas are financially feasible… for us and for others.

As the insightful quote above points out, we may have a bright idea, but if it doesn't have a bottom-line benefit, it has limited value.

In this section, you'll discover a variety of ways to assess your idea's real-world revenue producing potential to make sure it is worth pursuing.

CHAPTER 7
Assess Your I.D.E.A. for Equity Potential

*"Good ideas are a dime a dozen, and they're not worth
a plug nickel if you don't act on them."*
– Warren Reed (Sam's dad)

AS ALREADY mentioned, our goal isn't just to come up with ideas; it is to come up with ideas that have the potential to make money.

Karen, a participant in one of my seminars, put her hand up and said, "I'm one of those 'idea a minute' people. My problem is, I can't tell which ones are feasible and which aren't. Any suggestions?"

I said, "You're right, Karen. None of us have any spare time lying around. We can't afford to chase after ideas that won't pay off. That's why I've identified four ingredients an idea must have to warrant pursuing."

I've placed these four essential elements in an easy-to-remember acronym … I.D.E.A.

Next time an idea occurs to you, run it by these criteria. If it passes this test, it's probably worth exploring."

The Four Essential Elements of an Equity I.D.E.A.

I = INNOVATIVE

The very nature of an idea is that it advances or adds to what already exists. If it simply duplicates what is already available, then it's an observation not an idea.

Want to know one of my favorite examples of an INNOVATIVE idea?

A Hawaii dive shop had a problem. They were turning away a lot of customers (and potential income) because people had let their scuba certification lapse. These customers were upset because they had been looking forward to exploring the coral caves and immersing themselves in the tropical aquarium-like environment; but the dive shops had to enforce the rules which were "no certification, no scuba dive. A dive shop manager kept looking for a resolution to this money-losing situation and finally had a light bulb moment.

Why not run a air hose from the dive boat that people could put in their mouth, kind of like a long snorkel, so they could "swim with the fishes" to their heart's content. There wouldn't be any risk because people would only be about 10 -20 feet down so they could re-surface in seconds. People wouldn't have to cart around the heavy oxygen tanks and anyone could do this because they didn't have to go through the time-consuming, costly training.

What to call this new sport? Well, using a technique you'll learn in **Chapter 11: Combine the Best of Two Ideas to Create the Next New Thing**, the dive shop manager came up with the perfect name. It is half scuba and it is half snorkel … it is SNUBA.

Millions of people have now experienced the thrill of being able to swim in an underwater world, in a crystal clear ocean, uninterrupted, for up-to-an-hour at a time because this manager put one and one together – and came up with a new activity.

Cynthia Maller is another example of an IDEApreneur who was not content to be a copycat. As the former Global Creative Director for Yahoo, she was tasked with ramping up Yahoo Personals presence online. The challenge? Match.com had been first to market. And, **whoever is first to market usually owns the market.**

Cynthia started looking for a creative loophole. What could Yahoo Personals do that was different from what everyone else was doing? She had an epiphany. "Why not feature real people in our ads? In fact, why not feature satisfied clients in our commercials and web pages?"

This may seem like an obvious option now, but it was a radical notion at the time. The common practice in the industry at the time was to use fabulous-looking models to entice people to sign up for the service. The assumption was people would be motivated to register because they hoped to date someone that good-looking. Cynthia's insight was it was more important for people to be able to relate to the people in the ads. They wanted to connect with someone who "looks like me and who would look at me."

This innovative idea helped Yahoo grab market-share because now THEY were first-to-market with an offering people valued and couldn't find elsewhere.

Are you offering something people want and can't find elsewhere? If so, people will flock to you.

D = DELIVER RELEVANT VALUE

The earning potential of an idea can be determined by an almost mathematical equation. The bigger the problem someone has, the more urgent the need they have, the more unique your solution to that problem, the more value your idea will deliver, the more people will want it, and the more they're willing to pay for it.

A fascinating article in *Bloomberg* proves this point. The article reports that Facebook is now valued at 201.6 *billion* dollars as of September 2014. (yes, that's a b).

In 2015, CNN announced Facebook's market value was $245 billion (more than WalMart's). On Feb. 1, 2016, *Fortune Magazine* reported that Facebook is now valued at $315 billion, more than Exxon at $315 billion. That's an amazing feat for a company that's only been around since 2004 and started trading on Wall Street in 2012.

Which is all rather astonishing when you remember Facebook was founded by a college student. Mark Zuckerberg was sitting in his dorm room and thought, "Wouldn't it be neat for college students to have their own social networking site – a type of online yearbook?"

Zuckerberg's idea was simple – make it easy for people to set up their own online page to communicate with friends; share photos and videos, meet like-minded people, find out what's going on, swap opinions, connect with and join groups of people who have common interests.

More than a billion people use Facebook every single day, for an average of 20 minutes daily. Why is it so popular? Well, it does a superlative job of serving a purpose, fulfilling a need, and delivering relevant value. As one member says, "It's the one-stop shop for all my social needs. It's where all my friends hang out. There's no reason to leave."

Talk about delivering relevant value. Easy access and constant contact with people who care about the same things you do – for free. No wonder this Equity Idea has turned into a multi-billiondollar commodity that has scaled at an unprecedented pace.

E = EASY-TO-UNDERSTAND-AND-REMEMBER

This can be one of the most challenging steps of the process. It's one thing to have an idea YOU understand. It's another to be able to get it across in a way other people can understand it.

Simply said, if *they* don't get it, *you* won't get it. If people can't instantly grasp what your idea's about, they won't relate to it, remember it, want it or recommend it ... which means even if your idea is brilliant, it has little chance of gaining traction and breaking out.

IDEApreneur

In Chapters 16-18, I'll reveal several specific ways you can name and explain your idea so people get it and want it. For now, I'll share an innovative idea that hasn't lived up to its hype – at least partially because people didn't "get" its name.

Do you remember years ago when there was a lot of rumors flying around about a secret invention code-named IT or Ginger? Author Steve Kemper predicted that this new mode of transportation would "change the world," leading to much speculation and anticipation.

Then, inventor Dan Kamen, who also invented the first portable insulin pump, revealed his revolutionary new mode of transportation - a gyroscope-based electric scooter – his next new thing, a human transporter. What did he call it? *Segway*.

Seg-what?!

I can only guess this was intended to be a play on the word "segue" which means "leads to what's next." Kamen (and many people in the transportation industry) had high hopes for Segways. They predicted people would use them to get around town, reducing dependence on cars and eliminating pollution, traffic congestion, the need for huge parking structures, etc.

The problem? Most people aren't familiar with the word "segue." They don't use it and many don't know how to spell it.

Uh-oh. A prescription for disaster. This pioneering product was given a name that produced the deadly "huh?" response. A name people couldn't relate to or remember.

A name that caused people's eyebrows to crunch up – a sure sign of confusion. And as explained in my book *Got Your Attention?* confused people don't say yes.

That's a cautionary tale of what can happen when you fail to give your idea a name that's easy to say and easy to remember. A revolutionary invention that was predicted to be a game-changer never fulfilled its promise, at least partially because people couldn't pronounce its name.

There's an interesting twist to this story. A business in Washington DC realized that, especially in the hot days of summer, tourists visiting the national monuments, White House, U.S. Capitol, and Smithsonian get tired after walking for miles between these visitor destinations.

Hmmm. Why not rent Segway's and host guided Segway tours so people can get around painlessly and see more places in less time, with a docent? What to call this business?

Well, using a technique covered in Chapter 15, they played off the title of an enormously popular TV sitcom and came up with a fun name that earned it a place on my 2007 POP! Hall of Fame.

The name? *Segs in the City*.

Kudos. That's how it's done, folks. Giving their business a fun name generated millions of dollars of free publicity. The resulting visibility has made Segs in the City a thriving business.
So how about you? When you tell people your idea, do they look at you with blank eyes? Or do they light up? Do their eyebrows crunch up or rise up? If they can repeat your name after hearing it once, good for you. If they want to know more, congratulations! It means you got your idea's foot in their mental door.

A – ACTIONABLE

The fourth criteria of an Equity IDEA is that your concept can be turned into something concrete. The intangible needs to be turned into something tangible. The ephemeral needs to become empirical.

Ideas that remain in your head help no one. They don't have the power to make a positive difference for you and others until you transform them into a real-world offering.

In interviewing people for this book, I encountered countless individuals who had a "big idea," but never did anything with it. A colleague told me that years ago she got tired of lugging her heavy suitcase through an airport and thought to herself, "They really ought to put wheels on these things." Argghh. Who knows? If she had followed up on that idea, she could be a multimillionaire today.

Want to know my favorite example of someone who wasn't content to just think of an idea – he acted on it – doing himself and many others a world of good in the process?

13-year-old Jack McShane lived across from New Orleans' City Park. Unfortunately, the park was devastated by Hurricane Katrina and the resulting floods. City officials ended up abandoning the park because they had limited funds and were busy re-building infrastructure elsewhere.

Jack had grown up playing in the park and was bothered by it being so overgrown and unusable. He was looking at it one Saturday and thought, "*Somebody* ought to do something about it."

Then he realized, "I'm as much a somebody as anybody. *I* ought to do something about it."

He took his family lawn-mower out of the garage, walked across the street and started mowing. People complimented him for his efforts so he recruited some friends to help out. One of his friends was called Ron so they called themselves the Mow-Rons.

They even came up with a slogan, "The Mow-Rons are in City Park. The idiots are in City Hall."

That edgy slogan got Jack's cause a lot of national media attention. He had second thoughts about the slogan though because he thought it was "a little inappropriate" and didn't accurately represent his message which is the importance of taking responsibility to give back to your community. After brainstorming, they came up with the perfect name, *Weeding by Example*.

The media is always looking for feel-good stories. Jack was featured on *CBS Evening News* in a report by Scott Pelley, scaling visibility and donations for their non-profit.

Now ask yourself, would Jack's non-profit have gotten that national media attention (and additional financial support) if they'd had a confusing, clunky name?

Does your idea pass the IDEA test?

If so, kudos, you have an Equity Idea. If not, keep reading. The upcoming chapters show you how to create and monetize Equity Ideas that *do* have all four of these essential elements.

Questions to Ask – Actions to Take

1. **I – Innovative**. Is your idea unique, new, first-of-its-kind? How is it disrupting the norm?
2. **D – Deliver Relevant Value**. How does your idea solve a problem, meet a need, address an issue? How does it relieve people's pain or make them happier, healthier or wealthier?
3. **E – Easy to Say and Remember**. Can people explain/repeat your idea after hearing it once? Do their eyebrows crunch up because they're confused or go up because they're intrigued?
4. **A – Actionable**. How will you get your idea out of your head and into the world? How will people access it, try it, buy it and/or use it so it has real-world value and benefit?

CHAPTER 8
Complete a W5 Form to Make Your Idea a Mutual ROI

"Dullness won't sell your product, neither will irrelevant brilliance." – **Bill Bernbach**

REMEMBER EARLIER, we established that for an IDEA to have commercial potential, it can't be dull and it can't just be brilliant. It needs to:

- Innovative
- Deliver Relevant Value
- Easy-to-Understand-and-Remember
- Actionable

Another litmus test of whether an idea is an Equity Idea is whether it will be a mutual ROI (Return on Investment).

Best-selling author Scott Turow learned this lesson the hard way. Scott's books (*Presumed Innocent, The Burden of Proof,* etc.) have sold more than 25 million copies worldwide. Scott was asked, "What's been your biggest lesson as a writer?"

Turow considered this for a moment and then chuckled and said, "I once spent six months writing a book that was based on a legal precedent called the '*Law of Inhabitability*.' I turned my finished manuscript into my editor who got back to me a week later with some bad news. He told me, 'Scott, you may think this topic is fascinating – but nobody else does.'"

Argghh. Scott had to scrap the project because he had violated the cardinal rule of commercial viability, "We may care about an idea and think it's interesting. The more important question is, will our audience care about the idea and find it interesting enough to buy?"

If Scott's purpose was to sell books, his idea had to appeal to his fans. This premise didn't, which meant it wasn't an Equity Idea. NEXT!

Over the years, hundreds of people have consulted with me to create a one-of-a-kind equity brand and business, craft their presentation, develop their book, or grow their consulting practice.

One of the first questions I ask is, "*Why* are you pursuing this idea?" Reasons frequently given range from "I want to:

- Leave a lasting legacy and make a positive difference for people
- Become a nationally-known topic expert, thought leader and media resource
- Be an entrepreneur - my own boss – instead of "work for the man" Generate more revenue-producing business and attract new clients and more clients
- Do work I love that I'm good at – and get paid for it
- Do something about a problem or cause I care about

These are all decent reasons. But they're not enough.

The more crucial question is, "Why will people find your idea, information and approach interesting, useful, and worth their valuable time, attention, and money?"

How will your idea:

- Save *them* time or make *them* money?
- Motivate them or inspire them to take action on a priority project or goal?

- Prevent trial-and-terror learning and provide a short cut to success?
- Connect them with people experiencing the same challenge so they're not alone?
- Teach them how to acquire a needed skill?
- Point out how they're doing something wrong and show them how to change?
- Expand their horizons and give them experiences they'd never have otherwise?

All of the above are valid purposes for proceeding because they focus on how *other people* will benefit from your idea, not just you.

Clarify up front why your idea will serve people and keep that in mind as you proceed. Your intent to serve will be self-evident and people are more likely to care about what you have to offer and feel connected to you because they'll sense this is not an exercise in ego.

A participant in a program asked, "Can my idea have multiple purposes?" Another piped up with, "Do the purposes for our idea sometimes change?" … Yes and yes.

Vicki Falcone is a great example of this. Vicki wrote a intriguing book with the clever title *Buddha Never Raised Kids and Jesus Didn't Drive Carpool*. That stop-em-in-your-tracks title helped her get a good deal with a publisher (one of her purposes) and attract a lot of media attention (another purpose). The book sold well and was enthusiastically received by readers who found it full of good ideas they could use to parent more positively (another purpose).

However, the book didn't fulfill one of Vicki's most important purposes. Audiences loved Vicki's down-to-earth, witty yet insightful style and she had hoped the book would generate even more high-fee speaking engagements.

This is where the edgy title caused some problems. Some educational organizations and parenting associations balked at the religious references in the title, so, Vicki is re-titling and repositioning her books so they appeal to a wider spectrum of meetings planners, conference coordinators and program committees.

The point? When you get an idea – whether it's a title for a book, a new product you want to roll out, a direction for your business or a new service for your organization – it's important to ask and answer your W's.

What are the W's? As Robert Louis Stevenson said, "I have six honest servants; they've taught me all I know. Their names are What, Why and Who, When, Where and How."

Taking the time to do this exercise can help you get clear about your idea's What, Why, Who, When and Where – so you are completely clear as to why your idea is worth trying and buying and an ROI for your intended customers and decision-makers.

Your W5 Form – Your Drawing Board for Mutual ROI Ideas

"What did we go back to before there were drawing boards?"
– George Carlin

WHAT is your idea? Product to help people eat healthier? APP that helps people find their keys? Business that helps people design their own websites? Book on how to fund your startup?

WHO is your intended audience/decision-maker? What is their name, age, gender? What is their level of interest/ resistance with what you're offering? What are their problems? Needs? Objections? What is their mood? (Impatient? Eager?) Describe them so you can SEE them.

WHERE and WHEN will they access/use your idea? Every morning when they get up? At work – on their job? In their yard? Online anytime? When driving? In a hotel ballroom?

WHY will this be an ROI for your customers/decision-makers? Why will it be worth paying attention to, trying and buying? What are the "makes & saves?" How will this make and/or save them money and time, make them healthier, wealthier, wiser, produce bottom-line benefits?

WHY will this be an ROI for you? What 3 possible outcomes would make this a tangible success for you? What do you want people to stop, start, feel, do differently as a result of your idea – and if they do this – it's a win? What *measurable* results do you want to receive?

Want to hear a couple of my favorite success stories that show the importance of filling out a W5 Form?

A potential client had an idea she wanted to pitch to a well-known airline. A popular fitness guru, she wanted them to sponsor in-flight fitness videos and a TV show (starring her) on a travel channel.
I asked her, "Do you have a tagline or slogan yet?"

"Yes," she told me. "It's … *'Get out of your comfort zone.'*"

Yikes. I was on the airline's website. Guess what their slogan was? *Get IN Your Comfort Zone.*

That would have been a disaster. She could have spent a lot of time and money on her idea – and taken herself out of the game in the first 60 seconds of her pitch because what she was proposing flew in the face of their brand positioning and messaging.

That's one reason it's worth doing your W5 homework early in the process of developing your idea and *before* you approach your target customers and decision-makers.

Here's another.

I was working with an executive of a Fortune 500 tech company based in Silicon Valley. He had the idea to gather everyone in his division for an all-hands meeting and had just showed me his finished power-point deck.

I asked him, "How do you want people to feel at the end of your presentation?"

Blink. Blink. "Feel?"

"Yes. This is your annual all-hands meeting where everyone comes together to review the previous year and preview the ideas and priorities for the coming year."

"Well, I guess I want them to feel … *proud*. We not only hit all our numbers, we exceeded them."

"Okay, what else?"

"Well, I want them to feel … *excited*. We've got a big launch coming up in Q1 and I want them looking forward to it."

"Got it." I paused, then asked. "Do you think you might want to put some pictures of *people* in your deck?"

I'll always remember the look on his face. This had never occurred to him. He was a tech guy. His deck was filled with numbers, graphs and grids; but not one picture of a human being.

He was a quick study. The next day he asked the company photographer to go around and take pictures of the individuals who had put in the 60 hour weeks, put out the fires, and pulled off the miracles … and he integrated them into his deck.

He got in touch the next week to say, "Sam, you should have seen them. People were going around cheering and high-fiving each other. The mood and energy in the room was off the charts."

Kudos. That's the power of putting yourself in the situation and in the minds of your intended customers and decision-makers *in advance*. You can anticipate their objections and address/remove them early in your communication or product description.

You can identify potential distractions and remove them. For example, when I asked this executive what time the meeting would be held, he told me, "4:30 pm on a Friday afternoon."

Whoa. Everyone would have one foot out the door. I suggested he play upbeat music and promise the meeting would end right on time so attendees wouldn't worry about it running late.

It's shocking to me how many people will spend time and money on their idea's website, social media, marketing campaign, power point development … and NOT fill out their W5 Form.

Do this FIRST. It's one of the single best investments you can make in ensuring your idea will turn out to be a successful investment for you … and for your customers and intended audience.

Questions to Ask – Actions to Take

1. Did you take the time to fill out your W5 Form? Did it help you identify potential objections to your idea that you can address early on when describing and/or pitching it? What were they?
2. Does the time and place people will first learn about your idea affect their receptivity? Will they be distracted, exhausted, pre-occupied? How will this shape how you present your idea?

3. What were three specific reasons your target customers or decision-makers will choose to give you their attention, trust, support, account or money? What's in it for them?
4. What are three outcomes that would make this a success for you? You never want to just have ONE desired outcome, because if that doesn't happen, your idea is a failure. Identify several results that would make this an ROI to increase the likelihood that this will be a win.

CHAPTER 9
Identify Your P.O.D (Points of Distinction)

*"Before you build a better mousetrap, it helps to know if there are any mice out there." – **Mort Zuckerman***

A CONSULTING client who filled out her W-5 Form encountered an obstacle.

She said, "Sam, I have an idea about a business and book that addresses the issue of aging parents. The last year I've been consumed with taking care of my mom and dad, moving them into a supervised care facility, selling the home they've lived in for the past 50 years, distributing their possessions, dealing with health challenges, taking them to the doctor, paying bills."

"It's been non-stop. I'm passionate about this topic, but when I did a Google Search and logged on to Amazon.com to check out the competition, I found hundreds of businesses and dozens of books about this. Is this idea even worth pursuing if there's already a lot of competition?" Good for Deb for assessing the competition before she invested a lot of time, money and effort in her idea. If there's already a glut of business and books on this topic, it's going to be very difficult for her idea to break out and get traction – even if her business and book add value. She had run smack dab into the reality of the marketplace. Unless she's able to deliver something different or better that breaks new ground on this issue, she will struggle to succeed.

To paraphrase Mort Zukerman, before building a better mousetrap, (or pursuing an idea), we not only need to determine if there are any mice out there; we also need to determine if there are already *too many* mousetraps out there.

Have you researched your competition? Did you log online and type in your type of business, product or service to discover who's already operating in your industry, market and space? Did you do a search on your idea to see who else is speaking, writing, researching, addressing it?

Did you discover a LOT of other individuals and organizations are already doing what you want to do? Is your product already available, your book already written, your business idea already taken?

If so, it's not a foregone conclusion that this is a "bad" idea. You don't necessarily have to abandon the idea just because other people got there first.

You DO have to pinpoint several specific ways to deliver your idea differently so it's not an exact duplicate of what's already available. You DO need to figure out how to position, package and present your idea so it doesn't copy or replicate existing ideas.

How do you do that?

One way to do that is to do the opposite of the obvious. Here are several ways to make your idea unique, uncommon, and one-of-a-kind so it stands a chance in a crowded marketplace.

The first way to do this is to … **Do the opposite, not the obvious.**

What are your competitors' norms?

If you want to break out instead of blend in, *do the opposite of that.*

What won't your competitors offer? Offer it.

Where are your competitors located? Go where they aren't.

For example, Enterprise wanted to enter the car rental business but Hertz and Avis owned that market. So, Enterprise asked themselves, what do our competitors have in common? Well, they're all situated by *airports* – so Enterprise located their rental centers in *neighborhoods*.

What didn't Hertz, Avis, Dollar, and Alamo offer? No pick up or drop service – so Enterprise introduced a first-of-its-kind service, an offer to pick you up and return you to your home, hotel or workplace.

Enterprise not only *broke into* a "saturated" industry, they broke out of it. Enterprise is consistently ranked as one of the top agencies in that multi-billion-dollar industry because they successfully identified two specific P.O.D.'s – Points of Distinction.

Another way to do the opposite, not the obvious … *is to lighten up*.

Art Buchwald said, "I learned when I made people laugh, they liked me."

Read your idea's description, web copy, pitch/proposal for funding and marketing material.

Does it make you smile or laugh? If not, it may be costing you sales. If you want to increase likability and memorability, inject some humor into your communications.

Follow the examples of the Super Bowl commercials. Every single year, the breakout ads that create buzz are the "funny" ones or the "touching" ones. The most popular commercial of 2016's Super Bowl was Hyundai's ad featuring comedian Kevin Hart "lending" his brand new car to his daughter's date, safe in knowing its tracking system would allow him to know exactly where they were and what they were doing. (It's funnier in the viewing.)

Humor can play such a crucial role in winning buy-in to your idea, I've dedicated a whole chapter to it. Check out Chapter 16 for specific ways to include true humor (not jokes) when pitching, describing, and explaining your idea so people are more likely to like it and you. Want a quick example of how you can use humor to give you a likeable competitive edge and differentiate you from competitors who take themselves way too seriously?

I stopped in at an ice cream store and laughed out loud when I saw this sign posted by the cash register. **"Why do we have square containers? Because we don't cut corners on the quality of our ice cream."**

I asked the young woman behind the counter if there was a "story" behind the sign. She told me, "We got asked that question all the time. We got so tired of answering it we asked ourselves what we could do. One of my co-workers came up with the idea for that sign. Ever since we put it up, it gets laughs and we don't have to answer the questions anymore."

Kudos.

Another way to do the opposite, not the obvious … *is to turn your idea on its head.*

Remember the Heinz catsup example I used earlier? They literally turned the industry and their product upside down in order to distinguish themselves from their competitors and become the next new thing.

Target did the same thing a few years back with an upside-down Christmas tree. Yup, they put the pointy part on the bottom (what, no star?) and the wide part at the top.

Their reasoning? More room for presents! Of course, this first-of-its-kind product generated a ton of free press because it was something people hadn't seen before. It also generated a ton of be-the-first-on-your-block-to-have-one sales.

Another way to do the opposite, not the obvious ... *is to be an "UN."*

Ask yourself, "How are my competitors alike? How can I be UN-like them?" This is what 7-Up did. Instead of going head to head with Coca-Cola and Pepsi, they offer a clear option to the dark sodas and became the UN-Cola.

WASH radio station in Washington DC also figured out a way to be an UN. Their marketing team observed that other stations were playing the same top 40 hits, again and again. To offer an alternative, WASH promises listeners they'll never play the same song twice during working hours. Their advertising slogan is, "We're the DO NOT REPEAT AFTER ME radio station." This claim to fame has helped them attract listeners tired of "same old, same old' and their rankings have increased as a result.

Another way to do the opposite, not the obvious ... *is to reverse an industry norm.*

For example, in the 60's, Detroit car makers Ford and GM were turning out large, luxury automobiles. So, Volkswagen went small. They figured there were consumers out there who didn't want or need a station-wagon or a four door sedan so they introduced the "Bug," a 2-door for budget-minded people (i.e., college students and young adults).

Volkswagen didn't stop there. Their creative team had the bright idea to emphasize their P.O.D. in self-deprecating ads that played off their small size and turned it into a proud, viable option to gas-guzzlers. One of their most famous ads featured a full page with 75% white space. A tiny Volkswagen Beetle was located in the lower right hand corner with this one-sentence caption:

"It makes your house look bigger." Well done.

One final way to do the opposite, not the obvious ... *is to ZIG where your competitors ZAG.*

Anita Roddick, founder of The Body Shop, said in an interview, "I watched where the cosmetics industry was going and then walked in the opposite direction."

Concerned about the animal testing that was standard in that field, Roddick insisted that none of their products involve experimenting on animals. Distressed over the toxic chemicals normally used in the manufacturing process, The Body Shop prides itself on natural, organic ingredients.

The cosmetic industry is known for its huge profit margins. A designer lipstick, skin cream, eyeliner, perfume or blush that sells for $50-$150 often costs less than a tenth of that to make. To counteract this perception of corporate greed, Roddick committed to donating a large percentage of their profits to third world countries.

She spoke frequently at conferences about social responsibility and modeled that one way to distinguish yourself from your competitors and win brand and customer loyalty for your idea, products and organization is to model integrity in a business that isn't known for it.

Questions to Ask – Actions to Take

1. Have you researched your competition? Is your idea original or first-of-its-kind? How so?
2. If you have competitors, what are your P.O.D.'s that differentiate you so customers and decision-makers have compelling reasons to support, buy YOU instead of the other guys?
3. How are you going to do the opposite of the obvious in your industry or profession? Name two ways you are going to be an UN or reverse an industry norm so customers will notice you and value how you're different or better than other options?

SECTION III
Turn Ordinary Ideas into One-of-a-Kind Ideas

"80% of life is showing up." – **Woody Allen**

WHEN IT COMES to your idea, 80% of its success is showing up *… first.*

It's not enough to simply show up with an idea.

If there are already products like yours, businesses like yours, services like yours, ideas like yours, it will be almost impossible to get noticed because you'll blend in.

This section shows how to turn everyday ideas into one-of-a-kind ideas that break out.

It shows how to give your ideas stop-em-in-their-tracks names, slogans and elevator speeches that motivate busy people to pay attention to what you have to say and sell.

A premise of this section is that people are busy. As mentioned earlier, they are bombarded with information and have the attention span of a goldfish.

So, it takes something special to stand out of the INFObesity – the glut of information 24/7 – and get noticed.

The techniques you're about to learn can help you do that.

CHAPTER 10
Turn Your Idea into a Trademark-able Term

"When you can do a common thing in an uncommon way, you will command the attention of the world."
– George Washington Carver

MY PREMISE for creating one-of-a-kind ideas is, **"The best way to corner a niche is to create a niche … and the best way to create a niche is to coin a brand new word."**

By coining a brand new word, you don't just have a trademark-able term, you have the beginnings of an evergreen business empire.
When you coin a one-of-a-kind word, you create your own playing field. Your original word can be legally owned if you can prove to the U.S. Patent Office that that idea, product, or word didn't exist before you created it.

And once you trademark, patent or copyright your idea, you can earn money from it … *in perpetuity.*

I'm speaking from experience (so to speak).

In 1981, I presented a workshop on the topic of conflict resolution for the University of Hawaii, called, *Dealing with Difficult People – Without Becoming One Yourself.*

Now, that's a catchy title. It's alliterative and it's got a beat that makes it easy to repeat (more on that in Chapter 18).

However; if you Google the phrase "difficult people," thousands of entries come up. That means I would have been competing with thousands of other individuals and organizations all addressing the same topic. It would have been tough to build a profitable business because of the sheer volume of specialists on the same subject.

Thankfully, an interaction in that first workshop triggered an IDEApreneur epiphany that took my business to a whole new level.

Here's the story. At the first break, a gentleman in the front row didn't even get up to get some fresh air or a cup of coffee. He just sat there, gazing off into space. I was curious so I went over to ask, "What are you thinking?"

He said, "Sam, I'm a real estate broker. I took this seminar because I deal with some very demanding and arrogant people. They seem to think they can treat me any way they want to. I'm tired of it. I thought you'd teach us some zingers to fire back at difficult people so we could put them in their place. That's not what this is about, is it?"

I agreed and assured him that giving people a piece of our mind was not the purpose of the program. The goal was to give ourselves peace of mind by being able to think on our feet and handle conflicts with compassion instead of contempt.

He continued, "I'm a student of marital arts. I've studied karate, taekwondo, judo. What you're suggesting is kind of like a verbal form of kung-fu, isn't it?"

The light bulb went off in my head. "You're right," I said "It's kind of like a ... *Tongue-Fu!*"

Eureka. The perfect name. *Tongue-Fu!*® is martial arts for the mind and mouth. Since this was a newly-coined word, I was able to officially trade-mark it. As a result, I was able to:

- Obtain a top notch literary agent who approached me after hearing my title
- Land a lucrative contract with a major New York publisher (St. Martin's Press)
- Attract big name endorsers such as John Gray, Tony Robbins, and Jack Canfield
- Be honored with favorable reviews from *Publishers Weekly, Library Journal,* etc.
- Be interviewed on hundreds of TV and radio shows including *Jay Leno's Tonight Show* and *To Tell the Truth* where our *Tongue Fu!* team stumped the panel
- Win many foreign sales with such countries as China, France, Japan, England
- Be excerpted or quoted in *Readers Digest, Investor's Business Daily, Chicago Tribune, Washington Post, Dallas Morning News,* and *Cosmopolitan*
- Certify dozens of people to teach this trade-marked methodology around the world
- Generate "niched" books such as *Tongue Fu!® at School*
- Create multiple audio and video products that are sold back of room and online
- Get paid to speak for hundreds of organizations and associations including NASA, Genentech, Booz Allen, Fortune 500 Forum, ASAE, Boeing and Servicemaster

Why am I telling you all this? Because most of the above would probably NOT have happened if that idea hadn't been given a trademark-able title.

It could have been the exact same idea with the exact same content – but it would probably NOT have gotten a book deal, NOT have generated the media attention, NOT have resulted in being hired by Fortune 500 firms, NOT have produced ongoing income via certifications.

Face it, when meeting planners are trying to decide who to book to speak at their convention, who do they choose? Any of the hundreds of people speaking on a topic that all look alike - or someone who has a title that will, (as they say in the biz) put cheeks in the seats?

Who do TV and radio producers choose to put on their shows? Any of the thousands of resources who are saying pretty much the same thing? Or someone with original, attention-grabbing approaches their viewers and listeners haven't encountered before?

A proprietary, trade-marked, one-of-a-kind name gets your idea's foot in decision-makers' mental door. It helps you POP! out of the pack. Are you thinking, "Okay, I'm sold. But HOW do I create an original term for my idea people haven't heard or seen before?" Here's how.

Get out a piece of fresh paper and list at least ten words you frequently use when explaining your idea to someone. How do you normally describe your idea to a potential client or decision maker?

And yes, you can do this on your computer too – although I find it kick-starts the creative process to make this a kinesthetic exercise and write the words vertically on paper so you can see them and move them and "doodgle" a variety of combinations from them.

For example, if you have an idea on how to increase retail sales you could write down discount, selling, mark-down, up-sell, save, money, opportunity, incentive, persuade, market, bonus, shop.

Those are your "core" words. They represent and articulate the core essence of your concept.

Now, take each of those words, one by one, and "talk" them through the alphabet, changing the sound of the first syllable to match the corresponding letter. Keep your antenna up for any words that sound intriguing, fun or relevant that have the potential to create a viable new variation.

IDEApreneur

For example, Tongue Fu! was an alphabetized form of Kung Fu. Don't stop there though; there may be other one-of-a-kind options if you keeping "talking" your word phonetically through the alphabet. For example:

Aongue Fu, Bongue Fu, Congue Fu , Dongue Fu

Eonge Fu – (*nope*, nothing yet)

Fongue Fu – (hey, how about Fun Fu! - how to handle hassles with humor?)

Gongue Fu! (Tongue Glue – how to hold your tongue so you don't say something you regret?)

Hongue Fu , Longue Fu , Mongue Fu

Nongue Fu – (*keep going*)

Oongue Fu, Pongue Fu

Rongue Fu – (This could be turned into Run Fu! – for when Tongue Fu doesn't' work!)

Songue Fu – (I could do a workshop on Tongue Sue – Tongue Fu for Lawyers)

And there's Young Fu – Tongue Fu!® for Kids!

And so on. Run Fu, Young Fu, Tongue Glue, Fun Fu! could be turned into merchandise such as t-shirts, coffee mugs, posters, calendars with quotes.

Those names could be used as chapter titles in a book, (which is exactly what I did in Tongue Fu!). Why stop there. They can also be turned into special reports (more on that in Chapter 23) tele-conferences, podcasts or presentations tailored to a specific audience.

These are all marketable-money-making ideas – conjured up for FREE with a little brainpower and the Alphabetizing Technique.

You don't have to have a crack marketing team or a million-dollar budget to come up with a million-dollar name. All it takes is this technique (and the others in this book) and you and your team investing a few minutes to run your idea's core words through the alphabet to generate first-of-its-kind terms you can trademark.

Want to hear one of my all-time favorite examples of how to originate a name that helps you and your idea get noticed … for all the right reasons?

A hotel restaurant/bar near Washington DC had a problem. No one was coming to their happy hours. Why? There were fifty restaurants/bars in a three-mile radius sponsoring happy hours. No wonder they were losing money; they were one of many.

As stated before, we don't want to be one of many. We want to be one-of-a-kind. When we're one-of-a-kind, we have no competition.

The enterprising owner kept his antennae up for a customer need that wasn't being met. He had an epiphany one day when he noticed that one of their loyal customers tied up his dog outside while he came in for a cold one after work.

Light-bulb moment. Why not offer a special happy hour for professionals who wanted to go for a walk after work with their poor pooch who had been cooped up all day? The bar could put out water bowls, hand out dog biscuits and offer a discount on beer so it was a win for everyone.

What to call this? Well, Alphabetize the core words "happy hour" through the alphabet, "Aaapy Hour, Bappy Hour, Cappy Hour, Dappy Hour" … and you eventually get to **Yappy Hour!**

You may be thinking, "Big deal, so it's a clever name."

You bet it's a big deal. *The Washington Post* wrote an article about the throngs of people showing up for the wildly popular (and profitable) Yappy Hour. That article was picked up by a hundred newspapers across the country. As a result, millions of people now know about the Alexandria, VA Holiday Inn's successful Yappy Hour, and they're thronged with customers who have made their Monday-Friday event a popular and money-making success.

General Mills and Yoplait had an idea for a new food product for busy people. They wanted to package yogurt in no-muss, no-fuss squeeze tubes so you could eat it on the run (in your car while chauffeuring kids, grabbing a quick lunch at your desk, dashing out the door to school) instead of having to sit down and spoon it out of a plastic carton.

They knew this was a great idea – they just needed to figure out what to call it. Look what happens when you "Alphabetize" the core word – yogurt.

Ao-gurt (*nope*)

Bo-gurt

Co-gurt (*keep going*)

Do-gurt

Eo-gurt (*not yet*)

Fo-gurt

Go-gurt (there it is)

Gogurt! It's close enough to the original so you instantly understand it -- and it also imprints the purpose of the product – it's yogurt for people on the "go." It's a new trade-markable word so they created and cornered a new niche and a multi-million-dollar product. That's the power of being an IDEApreneur who turns ideas into income.

I keep my antennae up for current examples of Alphabetized names and featured some of the best ones on my website, www.SamHorn.com. Some recent examples include:

- Flight-seeing (pontoon planes in Alaska that take tourists inland to see the terrain up close, landing on wilderness lakes
- Flickipedia (an online directory that describes popular movies)
- Yattle (a low-fat alternative to beef, a result of breeding cattle with Yaks)
- Suessical (a musical based on, what else, Dr. Seuss)
- Aristobrats (rich kids with an annoying sense of entitlement)

How about one more story to show why "Alphabetizing" is such a great way to generate a brand new name for your brand new idea.

Pulitzer prize-winning humorist Dave Barry (who endorsed **POP!** as "excellent advice for standing out from a crowd") writes an annual column in December describing quirky gifts his many fans have brought to his attention.

A crowd-pleaser was the item created by a father whose toddler loved to play "horsie." In case you're wondering, "horsie" is when a parent gets down on his knees and hands and "gallops" around the living room with his child on his back. The problem was, this father's toddler kept falling off.

IDEApreneur

Hmm … problem (the source of many great ideas). What could he do to help his toddler stay on? Well, how about strapping a "human saddle" on his back so his toddler could ride to his heart's content without worrying about toppling off?

What to call this contraption? Talk the idea's core word "saddle" through the alphabet.

Aaddle. (*nope*)

Baddle, Caddle

Daddle (tah da!)

Are you thinking, "So, Daddle is a cute name. So what?!" If you had taken the same idea and given it a boring name (i.e., human riding device), it never would have gotten off the ground (sorry). A blah title elicits a blah response. If your idea has an uninteresting name, people will yawn and move on.

By giving his invention a clever, concise, compelling name, Daddle came to Dave Barry's attention. As a result of being included in Dave's syndicated column (which is featured in hundreds of newspapers across the United States), millions of people know about Daddle (many of whom probably checked out the website and bought a Daddle for their children or grand-children) … all because this enterprising father made the effort to give his idea a name that got it noticed, for all the right reasons.

When you come up with a new word, be sure to "Google" it and search for it online and on Amazon to see if anyone else got there first. If no, pursue trade-marking it with USPTO. You'll find more specific details on that in Chapter 18.

Questions to Ask – Actions to Take

1. Have you given your idea a name yet? Does it elicit interest or cause confusion? Explain.
2. Would you like to give your idea a name that turns it into an evergreen business empire?
3. Start by writing down 10 key or core words that you use when you describe it to others. Now, run each of those words through the alphabet, changing the sound of the first syllable to match the corresponding letter. Be sure to write down any and all options, even if they're not perfect. Playing with all the options instead of immediately discounting them can lead to a one-of-a-kind NERD – New Word – that you can trade-mark and earn money from in perpetuity.

CHAPTER 11
Create the Next New Thing by Combining the Best of Two Ideas

"Creativity often consists of merely turning up what is already there." – **Bernice Fitzgibbon**

WANT GOOD NEWS? You don't have to "think up" an idea from scratch or sit around and wait for creative lightning to strike.

As Ms. Fitzgibbon pointed out, you can look at ideas that already exist and re-arrange or blend them to create an enticing new combination. How? Here's how.

Combine two aspects of your idea into a brand new "blended word." I'll give a couple examples first and then show you how to do it.

I drove by an old-fashioned theater a few days before Halloween and laughed out loud at the movie marquee. They were showing the ever-popular *Rocky Horror Picture Show*.

In case you're not familiar with this fan favorite, people dress up as their favorite character, sing along with the tunes, throw rice at the wedding scene, and get up in front of the screen and act out their favorite parts. What caught my attention was what they called this. It's half movie – it's half karaoke … It's MOVIE-OKE!

I guess you can see why I call these **"Half and Half"** terms. Combine a portion of two different ideas and voila! – you have just minted a brand new term.

People are always on the lookout for the Next New Thing. They're yearning for something fresh; hoping to be introduced to something they haven't seen or heard before.

If you want your idea to be the Next New Thing, start mixing and matching its different aspects to see if you can coin a completely new term that helps your idea break out instead of blend in.

Dr. Francine Kaufman, a pediatric physician, coined a new "Half and Half" term for a health issue that has reached near epidemic proportions. She said, "A decade ago, if I saw a child with Type 2 Diabetes in my office, it would have been so rare I would have written it up in a medical journal. Now, not a day goes by where I don't see several children with that diagnosis here at Children's Hospital in Los Angeles."

Studies have shown the link between diabetes and obesity for years. No one linked those two concepts in language though until Dr. Kaufman did. If you take the first half of "diabetes" and the second half of "obesity," what do you have? **Diabesity**.

You may be thinking, "Okay, that's nice, but how did Dr. Kaufman monetize that word?"

Guess who is now asked to speak at medical conferences around the world on this topic? Guess who the media wants to interview on this important topic? Any of the thousands of physicians or nutritionists who are addressing this issue? No, meeting planners invite and pay - and journalists call to interview - Dr. Kaufman, the individual who coined the term that put a name to this health crisis that's become an increasingly worrisome cultural phenomenon.

In the hyper-competitive meeting industry, program planners have the daunting task of trying to convince decision-makers to bring their conferences to their city ... when they have dozens of other options.

IDEApreneur

I had the opportunity to speak for MPI (Meeting Planners International) and met the Marketing Director for Seattle's CVB.

Stephanie told me Seattle hit the jackpot by coining an original term that's been featured in hundreds of newspapers across the country. Stephanie estimated their clever "Half and Half" name has reaped a billion dollars (yes, that's a b) in free publicity. The term – **Metro-Natural** – cleverly captures the dual nature of the city's cosmopolitan yet park-like setting. Well-done.

Fusion restaurants are a big fad right now. Fusion restaurants blend different ethnic foods to offer a new cuisine combination. For example, if you wanted to feature a menu with Chinese and Italian foods, what could you call it? Write down common Chinese terms and common Italian words and start mixing and matching them to create a word that indicates the meal will be a little bit of both. How about **Ciao Mein**?

How about a half Indian – half Hawaiian restaurant? **Taj Mahalo**.

Want one more example of the power of an original Half & Half Word to help you and your idea get noticed – for all the right reasons?

A fairly common occurrence these days is for twenty-somethings to move back home to live with their parents. There seems to be a lot of reasons for this – they're still paying off student loans, they can't find a job that pays enough for them to be self-supporting, or they can't find a job, period.

What are these kids called? (I love to ask this question in my public seminars because some jokester will always call out, "Losers! Free-loaders!")

They're often called Boomerang Kids. If you wanted to build a coaching business, write a book, or become a keynoter on that topic, featuring that phrase poses a problem because it is a generic, public domain word. It's what everyone uses. So if YOU use this word in your titles, you're going to sound and look like everyone else.

Remember, you don't want to sound and look like everyone else. You want to stand out. If you tried to build a career as a thought leader on this idea, you'd have a tough time standing out and making any money because you'd blend in.

If you really cared about this topic and wanted to wrap a living around it, you'd have to come up with a fresh approach so you'd break out instead of blend in.

Ian Pierpoint did just that. Think about it. These twenty-somethings are half...adults. I mean they're over 21. They can vote, drink, drive, even go to war. They're also...adolescents. They're living at home. Mom often does the cooking, the laundry, even picks up after them.

Join the two words "adults" and "adolescents" together and you have a brand new name for your idea – ADULTESCENTS.

Bingo. That's a six-figure book deal. That's a keynote address at the annual association for psychologists. That causes TV and radio producers to contact you. All because this IDEApreneur coined a new term that belonged to him and made him the instant go-to expert.

Half and Half ideas are almost guaranteed to stand out in the crowd – because there is no crowd.

When you coin a new term for your idea – you go to the head of the class.

You are the one who will get contacted by the media. *You* are the one who will get quoted in newspapers, profiled in magazines, hired to speak. You're the one positioned to monetize that idea because you coined an original word that positions you as *the next new thing* and pops you out of the pack.

Please note: in your marketing material, on your website, and when writing about your idea, by all means USE the words your target customers use when talking about this issue in the BODY of your content or in the SUB-TITLE of your work.

Deliberately using the most common words associated with a topic will bring you up in SEO when people are searching for advice on that issue or looking for solutions to that problem.

That's smart. Just be sure to feature your attention-grabbing word in the headline so it pops off the page and motivates people to check it out because they are intrigued and want to know more.

Questions to Ask – Actions to Take

1. Do you have a favorite "Half and Half" word that caught your attention and motivated you to check out a restaurant, clink on a link, buy a product or attend a conference session? What is it?
2. Get out a piece of paper, put a vertical line down the center of the paper, and start putting some of your key words in the left column, some of your key words in the right column.
3. Now, start mixing and matching them to see if you can create new combinations. Remember to write down any and all options. Do this exercise with a couple of colleagues and have someone say the options out loud so others can "riff" off them. Have fun. Remember, a process that takes a few minutes could result in you coming up with your own version of IDEApreneur.

CHAPTER 12
The Secret to Turning Generic Ideas into Genius Ideas

"Everyone is a genius at least once a year. The real geniuses simply have their original ideas closer together." – **G. C. Lichtenberg**

WHAT DO GOOGLE, Roomba, Boppy, Snuba and Yahoo all have in common?

They all are fun, easy-to-say-and-remember names that made their companies millions.

As we've established, what you call your idea matters. If people don't immediately understand it, they'll move on.

That's why it's crucial to give your idea a catchy name that stops people in their tracks and makes their eyebrows go up.

What's this about making people's eyebrows go up? It is a tangible way to check the commercial viability of your idea – anytime, anywhere, for free.

Simply tell people your idea … and watch their eyebrows.

If their eyebrows knit or furrow, it's back to the drawing board. It means they're perplexed. And if people find our idea perplexing, we've got a problem.

Why? People are way too busy to take the time to figure out something that's confusing. If we don't quickly prove that what we're saying or selling is of immediate value, they will check out.

I wrote a whole book based on the premise of the Eyebrow Test called *Got Your Attention?*

That book has been endorsed by Dan Pink (*Drive*), Keith Ferrazzi (*Never Eat Alone*), Amy Wilkinson (*The Creators Code*) and Marshall Goldsmith (*What Got You Here Won't Get You There*) who says it's "a must for every leader."

I give the back-story of the Eyebrow Test in that book and introduce 25 new ways to get people's eyebrows up for our cause, company or creation.

The premise of that book is that CONFUSED PEOPLE DON'T SAY YES.

One of the reasons it's a *Washington Post* bestseller is because it shows how, in a world of INFObesity and impatience where goldfish have longer attention spans than we do, to create clear, concise, compelling communications that capture busy people's favorable interest.

The Eyebrow Test is an almost infallible way to test market the appeal of your idea. When we are intrigued, our eyebrows go up. It's a visceral almost involuntary indication of curiosity. It's our mind's way of saying, "Hmm, this is interesting, tell me more." It means this is an eye-opening experience for us. We're engaged.

Want an example of a genius name that almost always gets a raised eyebrow reaction – and that turned a commodity product into a multi-million-dollar competitive edge?

Do you have a favorite coffee shop you stop by on the way to work? Starbucks? Dunkin Donuts? Peets? Have you ever burned your fingers on one of their hot cups of coffee?

If so, you probably put one of those paper "thingamajiggees" around your cup to keep it from burning your fingers. Those are unremarkable, aren't they? Nothing special about them, right?

Well, they're commonplace as long as they have a common name.

But IDEApreneur Jay Sorenson saw what everybody else saw – and saw something nobody else saw. He turned those cardboard insulating sleeves (their official name) into a 15 million dollar a year business.

How did he do it? Remember the core words we asked you to write down for the Alphabetizing and Half and Half techniques? Do that for "coffee" and for "sleeve" and start blending them together to see if you can make an alliterative phrase.

Why is alliteration so important? Alliteration (words that start with the same sound) makes you instantly eloquent. It makes your words fit together smoothly and makes them easy to say.

If you mix and match your Core Words and nothing pops, start writing down synonyms for your Core words and keep experimenting until you come up with something that gels.

Let's see, what are synonyms for coffee? Latte. Cappuccino. Java. What are synonyms for cardboard insulating sleeve? Well, it's kind of like a coat. How about "coffee coats."

Hmmm, interesting, but not quite there yet.

What's another word for coat? How about jacket? That's it. **Java Jacket**.

Jay says, "Java Jacket has such a dominant market awareness that people who meant to call our competitors call us instead. **The trademarked Java Jacket name is worth more than our patents.**"

That's impressive. Would you like customers calling you instead of your competitors because they can't remember the competitors name, they remember YOUR name? Then give your idea a genius name. A genius name turns a generic commodity into a one-of-a-kind competitive edge.

Remember, you don't have to have an advanced degree to come up with genius names. Everyday people can do it – if they just put their mind to it.

For example, a simple item that was produced in 30 minutes and selected as the "#1 Baby Product of the Year" by American Baby magazine was "thought up" by a working mom.

The first day Susan Brown picked her baby daughter up from the day-care center, the owner suggested she bring in a pillow the following day so her baby could be "propped up" and watch what was going on around her. The day-care center owner explained this would keep her daughter happy because she would stay visually and mentally occupied.

Susan experimented with several different pillows that night but none of them worked very well. A bed pillow was too soft. A couch pillow was too hard. (Is this sounding like Goldilocks and The Three Bears right about now?)

Susan started brainstorming. Maybe she could create a new type of pillow that did a better job holding her baby upright. She went to her sewing machine and stitched together a C-shaped pillow stuffed with foam that nestled around her daughter and helped her sit up. She took her C-shaped pillow to the day-care center the next day where it was an instant hit. Other mothers begged her to make one for their baby. Other day-care centers wanted to buy them and this evolved into a multi-million-dollar business was born.

What to call this handy, U-shaped pillow? Well, this is a baby product and people like to talk baby-talk, (i.e., blankie, dolly, nappy). How about **Boppy**?

Boppy is the poster child of how an everyday idea can become an Equity Idea.

It was innovative. It didn't duplicate what already existed. It delivered real-word benefits by solving a problem. It had an easy-to-understand-and-remember name. Originator Susan Brown didn't just think of this idea, she took action and produced a product that continues to generate income years after she turned her idea into a reality.

If you're ready to take something unremarkable and make it marketable, give your idea an alliterative name. It has the power to turn a generic product into a genius product.

Want further proof of the power of alliteration to help your idea pop off the page or shelf?

Say these words out loud:

- Dunkin Croissants
- Roll's Jaguar
- Best Purchase
- Dirt Vacuum
- Weight Observers

They sound kind of clunky, don't they? They don't have communication charisma. They don't make your eyebrows go up or give you any reason to say, "Tell me more."

Now, make the above business names alliterative and say the following phrases out loud.

- Dunkin Donuts
- Rolls Royce
- Best Buy
- Dirt Devil
- Weight Watchers

Notice how words that start with the same sound are pleasing to the ear and mind? Please note: alliterative words don't need to start with the same letter – they just need to start with the same sound. Alliteration makes your language lyrical and gives your idea an instantly elegant name that feels complete. You don't want to fiddle with the phrasing. It feels "right."

Jamie Allison, a mother from Santa Barbara, CA decided to get back in shape so she could "look better, feel better, have more energy, and get that flushed face glow." She started out with the best of intentions but found there were many days she just didn't feel like going out on her own.

That triggered an idea. There had to be a lot of women just like her who craved company when working out. Why not form a support group for women who wanted to train for triathlons so they didn't have to go it alone? Joining up with running buddies would make exercising a lot more enjoyable.

Now, of course, the question was, what to call this idea? If she called it something mundane, people wouldn't be sufficiently intrigued to want to know more.

Let's see if we can come up with an alliterative name for this group. Well, these are mothers running, women exercising, moms moving... how about Moms in Motion? Boom.

Short, purposeful and appealingly alliterative. Jamie also came up with an alliterative motto of "Fun, Fitness, Philanthropy." Doesn't that sound and feel right? It covers the three goals of the group in three words. Well done.

Questions to Ask – Actions to Take

1. Have you created some intriguing name options for your idea? What are they?
2. Stumped? So far, have you come up with, as a friend likes to say, bupkis? If so, it's time to organize a group brainstorm. Invite some friends for lunch or dinner. Ask if they'll join you in some of these creative exercises to come up with the perfect name for your idea.
3. Provide paper and pen for everyone. Take 5 minutes to describe your idea, and ask everyone to write down the key words they hear, the intriguing words that pop out, the words you most frequently use, words that occur to them about your idea that you're not using.
4. Then, go through the creative exercises from these chapters – Alphabetizing, Half and Half Words, Alliteration – to coin new combinations that have the potential to capture interest and catapult income for your idea.

SECTION IV
Make Your Ideas Marketable and Memorable

"I have a hard time remembering three things: names, my keys … and uh, I forget the other one."
– Victor Borge

Do people remember your idea after they hear about it or see it?

If they can't recall it, how are they supposed to contact you?

How can they recommend your idea to others?

How can they track you down to hire you or buy your product?

This section shows how to package and present your idea so people can repeat it … which takes your idea viral, and turns them into word-of-mouth ambassadors for your idea.

CHAPTER 13
Re-arrange Clichés to Give Your Idea a Fresh Twist

"Avoid clichés like the plague." – **Samuel Goldwyn**

Michael Jordan, world-class basketball player, was also a self-confessed ball hog. Even he admitted it was hard for him to share the ball sometimes because he had more confidence in his ability to sink a shot than his teammates.

At one Chicago Bulls practice, coach Phil Jackson got impatient with Jordan and called him over and then called him out. "Come on, Michael," he said, "You had a teammate open under the basket. Why didn't you pass him the ball? You know, there's no I in team."

Michael smiled and quipped back, "Yeah, but there is in WIN!"

Kudos. See how re-arranging a cliché can get a chuckle?

People mentally roll their eyes when we use a cliché to describe an idea. As soon as we say, "It's nice to be important, but it's more important to be nice," they feel we're wasting their time because they've heard this many times before. They conclude we don't have anything new to say and check out.

Please understand I'm not saying the above statement isn't true; it's just not new.

If we want buy-in for our idea, we need to intrigue people and one of the best ways to do that is to provide an unexpected twist to a common saying. People's eyebrows will go up in delight because you zigged where they thought you were going to zag.

Imagine you're looking for a slogan for your idea's cause or campaign. As discussed before, write down all the Core Words you use when describing or explaining it. Now, go to www.clichesite.com and enter your Core Words one by one. Chances are it will provide you with a variety of clichés using your Core Words.

Don't stop there. Start replacing key words in those clichés with humorous or intriguing substitutes to create a fresh variation that trades off and twists the familiar expression.

For example, Avon is committed to helping find a cure for breast cancer. It sponsors "39.3 miles in 2 days" walks in which thousands of people have collected pledges for their participation. The money raised goes to support research efforts.

What to call these walks? Well, search the "W" category in a cliché or quote dictionary and you find "Good things come those who wait." Substitute Avon's key word and you come up with **"Good things come to those who ... walk."** Well done.

eBay hasn't hired me to consult with them on a brand tagline or marketing campaign, but if they did, (smile), I'd recommend they feature 60 second spots showing thrilled real-life customers proudly showing off their great "find," the deal of a lifetime, and the tagline would be, **"Go ahead ... make my eBay."** This, of course, plays off the famous Clint Eastwood movie one-liner, "Go ahead, make my day."

A great slogan for Hummer, the former military vehicle that appeals to iconoclasts, would be, **"Do you march to the beat of a different ... Hummer?"**

Is your idea to offer sales seminars? Well, you have a lot of competition. How are you possibly going to stand out from the thousands of other trainers, speakers, and marketing experts who offer programs on how to improve your sales?

One way to help your idea stand out is to target the pond, not the ocean. Instead of trying to cover the entire sales process and be all things to all people, why not specialize in a certain aspect of the sales process, the first ten minutes?

Let's see, what could you call this? Combine a couple of our techniques. Take a contrarian point of view and focus on how people do it wrong. Then put a twist on an iconic line "You had me at hello" from the movie *Jerry Maguire*, and you end up with **"You lost me at hello."**

You could use that as a title for a book, presentation, and online product that focuses on how to lose sales in the first ten minutes – and how to replace those deal-breakers with deal-makers. Voila. You now have a unique and needed niche in a very crowded market.

Another way to make your idea current is to capitalize on commonly-known song titles. For example, when the *Pirates of the Caribbean* was released as a DVD just in time for Christmas, the parent company created holiday-themed posters with a play on the classic "Deck the Halls." Their slogan? **"Wreck the halls."**

When an installment of the Star Wars trilogy was released the first weekend of July, the marketing campaign was, **"May the Fourth be with you!"**

Are you thinking, "This is just wordplay." You're right. This is wordplay; however, it's wordplay with a purpose. It's wordplay that can produce profits. If you want to win buy-in to your idea, invest the time and effort to name it, title it, or describe it in a way that cause potential customers to say, "That's interesting, tell me more."

Questions to Ask – Actions to Take

1. Go online to a quote and cliché dictionary. Take each of your key words, one at a time, and search to find quotes and clichés that contain that word. Keep playing with options until one pops and you come up with an intriguing way to describe your idea that gets eyebrows up.
2. You can also "riff" off an already existing quote (with attribution) to introduce your idea. For example, Jack Welch said, "If you don't have a competitive edge, don't compete." I shared Jack's quote in a blog and then said, "If you don't have a competitive edge, you CAN'T compete" and then shared several ways to create a compelling competitive edge to win buy-in.

CHAPTER 14
Make Your Idea Relatable by Articulating What Customers Want, Need, Feel, Say and Think

"The way to a man's heart is through his opinion."
– Malcolm Forbes

ANOTHER WAY to think up a tagline for your idea is to ask yourself, "What do people say when they're dealing with this issue?"

Say out loud what they're feeling and thinking. Write down what's going through their heart and head. That way, you're capturing their opinions and emotions around this issue.

Be sure to include these "conversational phrases" when marketing your idea because it's one of the best ways to make your idea's messaging resonate with your target customers. They'll relate to it and think, "That's *exactly* how I feel."

Want to make your marketing and messaging even more powerful? Ask yourself, "What do people feel or think about the product or problem I'm solving, but they wouldn't dare say it out loud? What is a sensitive issue they're afraid to admit or express?"

If you feature these "underground" emotions when explaining your idea, you will *earn* people's attention because you're addressing "elephant in the room issues" everyone else tiptoes around.

For example, Greg Behrendt, a script consultant on the HBO sitcom *Sex and the City*, was sitting in a plot meeting discussing a story line for an upcoming show. One of the women in the group started talking about the perfect date she'd been on. They'd had a magical evening and she was thrilled when this great guy asked for her phone number.

She sighed and said, "That was 2 weeks ago and he hasn't called." The other women were quick to sympathize and offer reasons why he hadn't followed up, "Maybe he's out of town. Perhaps he lost your number. He's probably just been really busy." Another one said, "Nah, he's got commitment issues."

Greg, the sole guy in the room, listened to all the rationalizations and excuses and finally couldn't help himself. He leaned in and said, *"He's just not that into you."*

As you may know, that phrase became the title of his bestselling book on the topic of dating. It also landed Greg in the national media spotlight and catapulted his career to a whole new level.

Greg went from being one of several writers on a show to having HIS OWN talk show. His six-word observation also became a movie and a meme that entered the lexicon where it was merchandized into everything from t-shirts to cards. Sum total? Greg made millions from a meme. That's the power of coming up with a phrase that makes people's eyebrows go UP.

One of the most satisfying aspects of my work is helping people coin titles, taglines and memes for their ideas and projects that help them break out. For example, Julie Jansen is one of

the country's best-known career consultants. She hired me because she wanted to give her book a title that would help it become a perennial bestseller like *What Color is Your Parachute?*

She said, "Sam, all the great titles, like *Take This Job and Love It*, are taken. How can I come up with something that helps my book pop off the shelf?"

I asked her two simple questions, *"What do clients say when they come to your office? What do you hear from your clients, again and again?"*

She thought about it for a moment and then said, "You know what they all say? *'I don't know what I want; but I know it's not this!"*

Bingo. That became the title of Julie's evergreen book.

Evergreen is what publishers call a book that sells and sells. Imagine yourself in a bookstore doing the bookstore shuffle (you know when you've got your head tilted, shuffling down the aisle, checking out the titles.) Or when you're online at Amazon or Barnes and Noble checking out titles on a specific topic.

Eight Steps to a Good Job. Career Techniques for College Graduates. Blah, blah, blah. Boring.

Then you see, **I Don't Know What I Want, But I Know It's Not This**. Wouldn't you be compelled to pull that book off the shelf, click on that link to find out more? Wouldn't you think, "That's exactly how I feel! This book's for me because the author understands me?"

That's the power of integrating your customers' conversational catchphrases into your idea's "elevator speech," title or marketing copy.

When presenting or pitching your idea, be sure to listen to what people tell you afterwards. Write down what's troubling them, what's touched them. Take notes of what keeps them up at night staring at the ceiling, what frustrates them, what they can't figure out. Be sure to notice trends, what you hear over and over. Feature those heartfelt admissions in your copy and people will be more motivated to connect with you and your idea and want to try it and/or buy it.

Questions to Ask – Actions to Take

1. Have you been writing down what people say when they discuss your idea? Are you including exactly what they say in your idea's promotional copy so it resonates *with* them because it came *from* them? If so, good for you. They're giving you the answers to the test.
2. What are some of the "elephant in the room" issues people think or feel about your idea? How are you incorporating that into your idea's marketing so you're tapping into how people think and feel about your idea *privately* – but may not feel comfortable expressing out loud?

CHAPTER 15
Craft a Tell 'n Sell Elevator Pitch for Your Idea

"My grandfather actually invented Cliff Notes. It was in 1952, and he was ... well, to make a long story short." –
Steven Wright

REMEMBER WHEN Andy Warhol said we'd all get our 15 minutes of fame? Well, in today's rush-rush world, we don't have 15 minutes to get someone's attention. We have less than 15 seconds.

I'm not making that up. As pointed out earlier in this book, Harvard researcher Nancy F. Koehn found that *goldfish* have longer attention spans that we do. Goldfish, nine seconds. Human beings, eight seconds.

As explained earlier, if we can't explain our idea in a small time frame, people will already have lost interest and moved on. People are simply too busy, distracted or impatient to give us their "time of day" unless we can quickly convince them we're worth their valuable attention. That's why it's crucial to make our idea's "story" short.

As a result, it is *our* responsibility to "Cliff Note" the description of our idea into a succinct charismatic sentence or sound-bite that captivates peoples' interest ... in under 9 seconds.

Sound like an impossible dream? Not if you link your unfamiliar idea to an idea with which people are familiar and fond.

The secret is not to try to *explain* your idea. The more you try to explain how your idea works, the more confused they will become. And remember, confused people don't say yes and they don't keep listening or reading.

Instead, link your idea to something your target audience already knows and likes. Ask yourself, "What is my idea like … with a twist?'

I learned the power of this concept while in Denver for a speaking engagement with my sons, Tom and Andrew. We had a night free, so we went downstairs to the hotel concierge and asked if he had any suggestions for a fun night out.

The concierge took one look at Tom and Andrew and said, "You've got to go to D&B's."

We were from Maui at the time and had no idea what he was talking about. I asked, "What's D&B's."

This wise young man did NOT try to explain what D&B's was. Imagine if he had said, "Well, it's kind of like a restaurant, but it's also a sports bar and they've got video games, and TV's, sometimes even bowling, and people go there to watch football or play pool. But families go there too to play indoor games. It's kind of like an indoor amusement park or carnival."

We would have looked at him in consternation and said, "Huh?" It's just TMI (Too Much Information.) The longer he talked, the more confused we would have become.

Instead, he paused, smiled and said simply, **"It's like a Chuck E. Cheese for adults."**

Boom. A perfect Tell 'n Sell Elevator Speech. Eight words and we knew exactly what it was and wanted to go there. By comparing D&B's (which

IDEApreneur

we didn't know about) to Chuck E. Cheese (something we knew and liked), he "told and sold" D&B's in one succinct sentence. They should have put him on commission.

So, what do you say if someone asks, "Tell me about your idea?" Instead of trying to explain your idea, ask yourself, "What is my idea like – that this individual likes?" If you compare your idea to something with which they're familiar and fond, the light will go on in their eyes and their eyebrows will go up. A sure sign of interest.

For example, Spencer Koppel knew from personal experience that techies and geeks often find it difficult to find a date. His idea was to produce a social networking site for pocket-protector types. His site doesn't feature the standard "hold hands, drink pina coladas and stroll along the beach" personal ads. They're more along the lines of, "Tall, Dork, and Handsome."

What did he name his website? **Geek 2 Geek**. What is his "Tell 'n Sell" Elevator Speech? It's **Facebook for Nerds**. Clever guy.

Robert Frost said, "All thought is a feat of association." You can create a Tell 'n Sell Elevator Speech for your idea by associating it with something potential customers already view favorably. You're trading off the respected track record and/or piggy-backing on its proven popularity – which takes your idea from "unknown" to "I get it and want it."

Author Amy Krouse Rosenthal is a shining example of someone who created an intriguing elevator speech for her idea. Amy had noticed that many first-time mothers were not confident about their parenting skills. Many didn't have extended family nearby to teach them how to handle their newborns so they worried constantly about whether they were doing it right. As a result, many had a high level of anxiety and tension they were passing on to their babies.

Amy's premise was that since babies don't understand language, they respond to their parents' temperament. If the mother is uptight, the baby will probably be uptight. If, on the other hand, the mother is calm and serene, chances are the baby will be calm and serene. Her book shows how mothers can be more tranquil so their baby will be more tranquil.

It just took me a couple paragraphs to explain that. And therein lies the problem. If we were at a PTA meeting, cocktail reception or Chamber of Commerce luncheon and I had tried to explain the idea of that book to you in the middle of the hustle and bustle of a crowded setting, you (and your attention) probably would have wandered off.

So, let's associate Amy's idea (It's important for mothers to be serene and calm) to something or someone with which people are familiar and fond. Who is someone famous for being calm, serene and tranquil?

How about Mother Teresa? Gandhi? Dalai Lama? Wait a minute. Dalai Lama has potential. Let's use one of our other techniques and "alphabetize" Dalai Lama. Dalai Ama. Dalai Bama. Dalai Cama. Dalai Dama. And so on, until there's ... **Dalai Mama!**

Tah dah! We smile and want to know more. The litmus test of a great title and elevator speech.

Remember, your idea's elevator speech doesn't have to TELL ALL. The purpose isn't to comprehensively describe everything your idea is about; it's to say just enough to intrigue people so they want to continue the conversation. Once they're intrigued – you can go on to ask if they know anyone who's dealing with this issue. Once they have an opportunity to tell you how this idea is relevant to them or someone they know, you can expand on how your idea works and it might be beneficial or timely for them.

IDEApreneur

The point is, associating the premise of Amy's idea to someone who is known for those characteristics, "Cliff Noted" her concept and provided a verbal shorthand that helped people instantly grasp her essence of her idea.

Want one more example?

I had the privilege of emceeing the Maui Writers Conference for 17 years, and headed up the non-fiction/business/self-help retreat the week before it. One of the many joys of working with participants in my retreat group was helping them position and message the idea behind their book so it would earn the favorable interest of agents, editors and publishers.

I'll always remember Wally, a marine biologist, who studied whale communication. To conduct his research, he would take a boat out into the Pacific Ocean off the Hawaiian Islands during whale season (December – March) and use a sonar device to "douse" for humpbacks. Once he heard their sounds and located a pod, he would listen to their conversations. After years of recording their unique sounds, he claimed to be able to "talk" with them.

Are you thinking this guy is one taco short of a combination plate? You're not the only one. Wally was legit, but was having a tough time getting interest in his book proposal because decision-makers thought it was a little "woo woo." His challenge? To crystallize his book idea into a brief sound-bite that established credibility and commercial viability for his work.

Well, using the Robert Frost approach of association, I asked him, "What movie is your idea like? What movie features a character who talks to animals?"

Well, at that time, there was *Doctor Doolittle* with Eddie Murphy. But since Wally's purpose was to gain respect for his work, comparing himself to a comedy was not strategically smart because it would not help decision-makers take his work seriously.

So, we kept playing. When Albert Einstein was asked how he worked, he said, "I grope."

Over the years, I've learned from first-hand experience, that the "perfect" title or elevator speech doesn't often show up right away. Sometimes it does, and that's a gift. However, if at first you don't succeed, keep playing, keep mentally groping.

What other movies feature a character who communicated with animals? How about *Horse Whisperer* with Robert Redford? Boom. That was it. Wally became **The Whale Whisperer.**

That worked because *The Horse Whisperer* was a bestselling book which became a blockbuster movie. In fact, the author, Nicholas Evans, received $6.2 million for the film and publication rights ... when his book was only half finished!

Comparing his work to the work of an author whose debut book had become a phenomenal success was strategic because it overcame their skepticism and caused them to wonder, "Could this be another first-time author who breaks out with a book that has a similar premise?"

Want to know how you can do this? Go online to www.IMDB.com (Internet Movie Data Base) and enter your idea's Core Words, one at a time. Up will come a list of movies with your core words in them. Start replacing the existing key word in the titles and taglines with YOUR idea's core words. Keep mentally "groping" and re-arranging words to see if you can come up with a sound-bite that "plays" off a popular title. With a few minutes of creative brainstorming, you could come up with a succinct sound bite that gets across your idea so people get it and want it.

Questions to Ask – Actions to Take

1. So, what movie or book is your idea "like" that people like? Write down their names and then start substituting your core words to see if you can come up with something that links your unfamiliar idea to a successful film or book project people already know.
2. Who is a person who is a walking-talking example of your idea, who embodies its characteristics? Now, start using the techniques you've learned from this book to produce a variety of potential sound-bites that link your idea with this person so the lights go on and the band plays and people instantly "get" and value what you're talking about it.

CHAPTER 16
Use True Humor to Win Buy-In for Your Idea

"I learned when I made people laugh, they liked me."
– humorist **Art Buchwald**

Study the signage, web copy, ads and marketing material for your idea. Do they make you smile? If not, they could be costing you sales.

One of the most popular articles I ever wrote was called "The 8 Biggest Branding Mistakes Businesses Make." It has been featured in publications and blogs around the world.

One of the Biggest Mistakes was that many individuals and organizations take themselves their idea and their branding efforts WAY too seriously.

As Buchwald pointed out, when we make people laugh, they like us. And when they like us, they're more likely to like our idea, product, service or business.

For example, when Coca-Cola launched Coke Zero, their goal was to convince consumers who didn't like the Diet Coke taste that this new option was the "real thing." This was not a petty issue. The beverage industry raked in $90 billion that year. As popular as the Diet Coke brand was, there were many soft drink fans who didn't like the taste and wouldn't go near it.

The marketing team's goal was to get across the point that people who loved the taste of Coke now had a viable calorie free option. Their clever ads, which made that point brilliantly generated a double-digit growth in sales. What's the humorous line that built so much buzz and helped their new product succeed? **"Tastes so much like Coke, *our* lawyers have contacted *our* lawyers."**

Want another example of how giving your product a smile-inducing name can help it break out? Turtle Island Foods, based in Hood, Oregon thought vegetarians deserved a chance to enjoy Thanksgiving turkey – without the meat.

So, they created a "half-and-half" name – **Tofurkey**™ – that generated millions of dollars of free media attention for their creation. As founder Seth Tibbott says, "We're fine with the fact that people think it's funny. People remember jokes."

The city of Cincinnati understands the power of laughing at yourself. It has an annual Running of the Wieners as part of its annual Oktoberfest-Zinzinnati festival. Dachshunds dogs wearing hot-dog-bun costumes race across a downtown square to win money for charity. The motto for this popular event? **Buns of Squeal.**

An entrepreneur client who speaks at industry conferences and writes a weekly blog told me, "I know humor is important and can help win buy-in, but every time I try to tell a joke, it falls flat."

I told him, "That's why it's smart to stay away from jokes. They often come across as forced or false."

He said, "Well, then, how can I integrate more humor when I'm explaining my idea?"

I said, "The good news is we all have funny things happen TO us and AROUND us. All you have to do is start noticing what makes you laugh that's relevant to your idea and use it (with attribution) to illustrate your point."

He said, "But I speak and write about serious subjects. Humor could be out of place."

I told him, "Here's the thing. People can only pay attention to serious stuff for so long.

They may understand our idea is important; but if it is complicated or boring and requires mental discipline, incentive or bandwidth they don't have; they'll tune out."

"But I don't want to risk alienating my audience or target customers."
"I'm glad you brought that up because it's another reason not to use jokes. Jokes are fabricated. At some level, people are wondering, 'If you made THIS up, what ELSE are you making up?' It makes it hard for them to differentiate when you are telling the truth and when you are not."

"So what do I do?"

"Use TRUE HUMOR so people can trust you. When you share real-life experiences that actually happened to and around you, you maintain credibility because you're not fabricating things."

He asked me, "What's an example?"

"Well, here's a story I use when talking about *Tongue Fu!*® to illustrate the idea that humor can be a saving grace. It usually gets a laugh and lightens the mood after discussing 'dark' topics such as what to do when people are yelling at you, manipulating you or being mean to you.

"I was in an airport heading to my gate on one of those long moving sidewalks. A very tall man, at least 7 feet tall, was walking the opposite direction. I couldn't believe it. The people in front of me were pointing at him and laughing. I thought, 'How rude, there's no excuse for that.' "When he got closer, I could see why they were laughing. He had on a t-shirt that said in very large letters, *'No, I'm NOT a basketball player.'*

As he went by, I turned to say something and burst out laughing. The back of his shirt said, *'Are you a jockey?'*

"I had to meet this clever young man so I jumped off the moving sidewalk and ran back to catch up with him. I asked, 'Where'd you get this terrific shirt?'

"He said, 'My mom made it for me. I grew a foot between the time I was 16 and 18 years old. I was really sensitive and self-conscious about it. I didn't even want to go outside because everyone had to make a smart aleck remark. My mom finally told me, 'If you can't beat 'em, join 'em.' This is nothing. I've got a whole drawer full of these at home. My favorite one says, *'I'm 6' 13" and the weather up here is fine.'*

"I told him, 'This is so smart. You are a walking-talking model of Fun Fu!'

"Now it was his turn to laugh. 'What's Fun Fu!?'

"It's based on a quote from humorist Erma Bombeck, *'If you can laugh at it, you can live with it.'*

'Oh yeah, I can relate to that. I used to get so annoyed when people said something about how tall I am. These shirts have made all the difference. Now I have fun *with* my height instead of being frustrated *by* my height.'

"That wise young man shows how humor can be a saving grace. Instead of being annoyed or offended, he chose to be amused."

My client said, "Okay, that's a fun story. But how do you tie that back in to your idea?"

"Good question. It's crucial to 'hook and hinge' the punch-line or point of an anecdote back to our idea so people understand how it's relevant and how it relates to them."
"Hook and hinge?"

"The 'hook' is the key phrase or take-away of your story. In this case, the hook could be 'have fun with it instead of be frustrated by it' or 'be amused instead of annoyed or offended.'

"You 'hinge' the take-away phrase back the audience and situation by asking several 'you questions' that motivate them to explore how this might apply to them.

"For example, I often ask, 'Is there something you're *sensitive* or *self-conscious* about? Would you like to have *fun with it* instead of be *frustrated by it*? Would you like some non-combative comebacks so from now on you can be *amused with*, rather than *annoyed by*, that situation?'

"Do you see, by using the *same words* from the punchline or point of your story and turning them into 'you questions,' people are now actively thinking how they can apply this insight in their own life. *That's* how to integrate humor into your idea's descriptions and marketing material so it's relevant … instead of trotting out a joke that sounds fake, feels forced or falls flat."

My client asked, "Can I use your 'Hook and Hinge Technique' when writing about my idea?"

"Absolutely. A master-mind buddy, Denise Brosseau, got a book deal from Jossey-Bass and spent several intense months working on her *Ready to Be a Thought Leader?* manuscript."

When doing the final proof, she realized it was a bit too serious and would be more intriguing if she added some true humor. I told her, "All you have to do is think about real-life situations that have made you laugh out loud in the past few months that are in some way related to the ideas in your chapters."

Bingo. Denise illustrated a number of her ideas with laugh-out-loud anecdotes, including this one, one of my all-time favorites.

Denise was shopping for a baby shower gift at a Babies 'R' Us store in Palo Alto, California, near Stanford University. While waiting in the check-out line, she was entertained by a couple in front of her who were discussing the confusing instructions on the box that said the crib they were about to buy had to be assembled from scratch. They nervously asked the cashier, "Will we be able to put this together ourselves?"

The casher asked innocently, "Do you have college degrees?"

"Oh, yes," the man assured her, "I have an MBA and my wife has a Ph.D."

The cashier smiled and said, *"Then you're going to need to hire someone."*

Bada boom.

Denise told me, "The cashier's response was so unexpected, everyone in the area cracked up. I weave that story into my presentations and it always gets a big laugh. More importantly, it supports my idea that advanced degrees can add value, but they're not a prerequisite for being considered a thought leader in your industry."

Denise is right. Unexpected responses elicit laughter. That's why, from now on, if something causes you to laugh out loud, *write it down*. Then, figure out how you can integrate it when describing, pitching, and marketing your idea to give people a respite from the "serious stuff" and to win their positive attention for you and your project.

IDEApreneur

Want to see an example of how to integrate humor into a presentation?

One of the most rewarding aspects of the TEDx talk I delivered on the topic of INTRIGUE is that people tell me they find it funny. People on Facebook have told me they show it in staff or board meetings of their business or non-profit because *people enjoy watching it* and it motivates them to STOP giving elevator speeches.

Why do they find it funny? Because I used a tip from *Pretty Woman* Director Garry Marshall. During the Q & A following his keynote at Maui Writers Conference, one of our audience members asked his secret to making movies that make people laugh.

He said, "When making a comedy, screenwriters and directors have a mantra, 'Laugh early, laugh often.' They deliberately put a laugh-out-loud moment in the first couple minutes to set a precedent. Research shows that when people laugh in the first few minutes of a film, they tend to conclude it's funny and are predisposed to see it as humorous from then on."

You might want to watch this TEDx talk with your idea team. Notice the Carrie Fisher (from *Star Wars*) quote in the first minute, *"Instant gratification takes too long,"* how it gets a laugh, how it's hooked and hinged to my idea, and how we're off and running.

Author Roger von Oech said, "Necessity may be the mother of invention, but play is certainly its father." Want more ways to come up with playful lines to help market your idea? Check out the websites Brainy Quote, GoodReads and Quote Garden online. Search "Funny quotes about ____" and put in your idea's core words. Up will come humorous quotes related to your topic.

For example, perhaps you're an accountant who has an idea on how to motivate people to prepare their taxes early, instead of waiting until the last minute on April 15. Now that's a serious subject. Nothing funny about that, right?

Well, go to your favorite quote site and start putting in your core words, including the word "procrastination" which is a synonym for waiting, which is what many people do when putting off their taxes. Or, buy a joke book like Judy Brown's *Joke Soup* or *Joke Stew* that features hundreds of one-liners from top comedians.

Look under "procrastination" and there's Judy Tenuta's line, **"My parents always told me I'd never amount to anything because I procrastinated so much. I told 'em, 'Just you wait.'"**

You could quote her to start off your blog, podcast or social media post, then hook and hinge the key word of her quote to your audience, "Are you WAITING to do your taxes until the last moment? Are you procrastinating on calling your accountant or tax preparer? Well …"

Then jump into why it will be in their best-interest to book an appointment today, not someday. That opening is a lot more likely to engage potential customers because you pleasantly surprised them with humor. They'll think, "Maybe this won't be so bad. I'm going to have to this anyway, and that's the kind of person I want to work with – someone who has a sense of humor."

Be sure to give credit where credit's due. It is not okay to "rip off" other people's humor. It is okay to "riff" off comedian's humor just as jazz musicians riff off standard chords to make new music. Just hold yourself accountable for always attributing one-liners to their originators. You might even want to include their website or Twitter handle so this is a win for them as well.

Questions to Ask – Actions to Take

1. Remember, when people are laughing, they're relating and remembering. How are you going to integrate true humor when describing your idea so people are more likely to like it – and you?
2. Ask yourself, "Is my idea serious, complicated, depressing or boring?" If so, how am I going to provide comic relief by "riffing" off one-liners (with attribution) to pleasantly surprise people so they pay attention to my idea and give it a chance instead of tuning out?
3. What's happened to or around you recently that made you laugh out loud? How can you hook and hinge that appropriately funny, real-life situation into your idea's descriptions and promotions so people relate to it, remember it and want it?

CHAPTER 17
Make Your Idea Sing and Swing

"It don't mean a thing if it ain't got that swing."
– Duke Ellington

- What company is associated with "Just do it?"
- What company is associated with "It's the real thing."

YOU'VE PROBABLY read or seen thousands of commercials in your lifetime. Yet, I bet you can probably name the sponsoring company of these popular slogans (two of the top ten jingles of the last 100 years, as selected by Advertising Age magazine.)

What's the point? It may have been years since you saw or heard these slogans; yet I'm guessing you were able to name Nike and Coca-Cola. Wouldn't you like people to remember YOUR slogan years after they first heard it?

That's the power of making your idea so memorable it remains TOP of MIND with people year after year. Your competitors' ideas and products are out-of-sight, out-of-mind, while people are still thinking about you, talking about you, taking you viral and generating income. If you want people to remember your idea; put it in a beat to make it easy to repeat.

Why? Think back to kindergarten. Do you remember learning nursery rhymes in a cadence such as "Little Miss Muffet sat on her tuffett (by the way, what is a tuffett?) "Jack and Jill went up the hill to fetch a pail of water. Jack fell down and broke his crown."

They don't call 'em nursery *rhymes* for nothing!

Rhythm and rhyme give our mind a hook on which to hang a memory.

This is not petty, it is literally life and death. Before you think that's an overstatement, consider this example.

The U.S. government was concerned about injuries in car accidents so it launched a public service campaign, posting "Buckle up for safety" signs around the country. The signs were pretty much ignored.

So, they went back to the drawing board. And this time they came up with something much, much better. *"Clickit or ticket."*

You may be thinking, okay so it's an improvement. Actually, it's a lot more than that.

The U.S. government tracked accidents over the next few months and reported that this slogan had actually increased *compliance* and *decreased injuries* in accidents. This proves that these techniques you're learning on how to make your idea more appealing and actionable – can have a dramatic effect on whether your idea is ignored or acted on. You can invest thousands (and much more) in website design, patent lawyers, social media marketing, branding consultants, etc. Be sure to invest an equal amount of attention on your idea's name, tagline and elevator speech.

Rhyme is sublime. Advertising professionals and creative agencies have used it for years to create taglines that stick. Shop 'til you drop. Beer here. Hot to trot. Pay Day. It works.

Want people to remember your idea? Play with options to see if you can craft its title or tagline into a easy-to-repeat cadence.

Abby Marks-Beale, an expert on speed-reading, told me her corporate clients were spending six or more hours a day online. They asked her to develop a new program teaching their employees to improve their

IDEApreneur

efficiency when using computers to do work.

Our first attempt at a title fell flat. *Increase Your Effectiveness on the Computer While Reducing Stress and Wasted Effort* didn't ring or resonate.

After trying a few different combinations, we came up with *Increasing Productivity Online While Saving Time, Frustration and Paper.*

Nope. It was better, but it didn't sing yet. We kept experimenting. How about **Increasing Productivity Online While Saving Paper, Frustration and Time.**

Wow. The same words in a different sequence produced a rhyme and cadence that made it POP! (And yes, it's a long title, but it is purposeful because Abby's clients want "meat," not "fluff" and this title tells them exactly what they're going to get for their money.)

Another technique that can make your idea's tagline memorable is to say it with a unique inflection – every time – to turn it into a signature line that is associated with you and you alone.

"If you see something, say something."

"What happens in Vegas, stays in Vegas."

"I can't believe I ate the whole thing."

If you're a boomer, you might remember a famous radio announcer who turned eight common words into a signature slogan by saying it with a … pause … and a particular emphasis on a specific word, every single time.

There are thousands of radio announcers in the United States. Yet Paul Harvey was one of the most popular – which translated into a larger salary, lucrative book deals and speaking engagements – because he was not content to be common. One of the reasons he stood out from his crowd was he took responsibility for giving people something to remember him by.

His signature phrase? *"And now ... (pause, pause, pause) ... for the rest of the story."*

Are you thinking, "How exactly does this generate a marketable, money-making idea?"

Take the example of boxing announcer Michael Buffer. He also turned a *common* phrase into a *signature* phrase. You've probably heard his trademarked (really!) line, "Let's get ready to …"

Did you say **"Let's get ready to … rumble?"** He actually gets royalties if you use his exaggerated inflection of that phrase for commercial purposes. That's the power of giving your idea a distinctive slogan that is said with easy-to-mimic-and-remember inflection.

I read a tragic article in *USA TODAY* about a toddler who was run over in his own driveway when his babysitter didn't look behind her when backing up. The child's parents wanted to bring this tragedy (which is more prevalent than you might think – there's more than 600 driveway back-over accidents a year) to the attention of fellow Americans so other families wouldn't have to endure a similar heartbreak. These parents formed a non-profit agency to spread the word about this issue and launched a Public Service Announcement campaign to raise awareness. What to call it?

Remember, the goal of a motto, slogan or tagline is to imprint the action you want people to take – so every time they *see* or *hear* your idea, they are reminded of what they're supposed to *do*.

IDEApreneur

Identify the verbs (action to be taken) and nouns (object of the action) and mix and match them until they fall into a natural rhyme or rhythm.

If you do this with the parent's cause (to prevent drive-way back-over accidents), sample verbs might be "see, watch, glance, look, search, spot." Sample nouns could be toddler, youngster, child, kid, baby, tot." There it is. **Spot the Tot**.

Why did I include this sad example in this book?

Because caring about your idea or commendable cause isn't enough. You want other people to care about it too.

If you have a worthwhile issue that deserves to be brought to the public's attention – it's *your* responsibility to communicate that idea clearly, concisely and compellingly.

I believe one reason this campaign is getting so much well-deserved press coverage is because the parents thought up an easy-to-repeat-and-remember name that got it noticed … for all the right reasons.

Let's make a mental shift here for one more example of the power of rhyme and rhythm to help an idea break out. I was in Seattle on a media tour and was impressed with how a local guidance counselor had used rhyme to "Cliff-Note" a complex idea into a memorable sound-bite.

It was prom season in the Northwest and parents and educators were concerned about the fad of "freak dancing." In case you don't know what that is, suffice it to say, it's when the girl has her back to the boy and, well, bumps and grinds against him. Moms, dads and school personnel were in an uproar. How would chaperones police this kind of thing? They could produce pages of regulations but that wouldn't help much when the music's on and they're trying to enforce a list of complicated rules.

I wish I knew her name so I could give her credit, but this savvy school counselor had the exceedingly smart idea to put the "freak dance policy" into a rap to make it hip and fun instead of punitive. Her brainchild? **"Face to face ... leave some space."**

Six words that condense that policy into an easy-to-enforce rhyming rap. Kudos to her.

Questions to Ask – Actions to Take

1. Think about your favorite cause or brand. What is its name and slogan? Has it helped itself stay top-of-mind by having a repeatable and retweetable tagline? What is it?
2. How about your idea? Get out your list of core words and your elevator speech and start playing with rhythm and rhyme combinations to experiment with different taglines that are easy to repeat and retweet. Remember, this isn't a waste of time; it's an investment of time that could be the difference between your idea getting traction or going in one earout the other.

SECTION V
Monetize Your Ideas with Ongoing Business Activities

"Money doesn't guarantee happiness; it guarantees options." – **Chris Rock**

OKAY, you have marketable, money-making ideas, now what steps can you take to start producing cash?

How can you turn yourself into a respected, in-demand IDEApreneur who gets paid to speak, paid to consult, paid to write on your idea?

How can you protect your Equity Ideas so you can profit from them for years to come?

How can you monetize your mind?

Our goal is to generate wealth - in all the ways that matter - by capitalizing on rich thoughts so they make a positive difference for others and a prosperous living for us.

CHAPTER 18
Be the Master of Your Idea's Domain

"A successful Imagineer has the imagination of a five-year-old and the wisdom of a grandparent."
– Walt Disney

UP UNTIL NOW, we've discussed ways to increase the flow of ideas and make them commercially viable by giving them compelling, strategically selected, on-purpose names and elevator pitches that will help them get noticed and bought.

The purpose of this chapter is to clarify that even if you do all the above, you don't have a commercially viable idea unless you have your idea's related URL and website.

Did you know E-commerce is crucial to your idea's success these days?

Did you know more people shop online now than at brick and mortar stores?

Did you know that when people hear about you and your idea, the first thing they do is to go to your website to "check you out?"

That's why it's essential to own your idea's domain name and have a professional website so you "own" that idea in the public's mind and can monetize your idea through online sales, services, programs, information products, etc.

To paraphrase Walt Disney, a successful IDEApreneur has the imagination of a five-year old, the wisdom of a grandparent, and the e-commerce savvy of Steve Jobs, Jeff Bezos and Mark Zuckerberg.

That's why, as soon as you form a name for your idea that has "brand" potential, your next step is to go online to your favorite domain register site (e.g., www.GoDaddy.com) to see if the corresponding URL is available.

If it is, claim it!

For $12.99 or less (at least that's the fee as I write this in 2016), you have reserved your idea's identity online. Protecting your intellectual property online is the equivalent of investing in real estate. You can breathe a sigh of relief because you have "staked" your claim on your idea's online home. As long as you pay the annual renewal fees, no one else can set up a website with "your" URL and proprietary phrase.

If you search for a domain name associated with your idea, and discover the domain register site is charging a "premium" price of hundreds and thousands of dollars, it's because they think it's a valuable site name they can charge more money for.

Before you pay a huge sum of money for a domain, get creative. I don't usually recommend getting .net or .info or .org UNLESS it is vital to have a domain with your idea's name, as most people automatically put in .com – even if they have your business card in front of them.

If someone else has an active .com site with the name you're using for your idea, you'll be competing head to head with them. They have name equity and you may be unintentionally sending them a lot of traffic.

An option is to add a word to your idea that turns your idea into a project or lab. For example, Pulitzer Prize winning columnist Ellen Goodman had a friend whose parents died without a will. The remaining siblings ended up fighting over the estate and their once close bond was ruined by the conflict.

Ellen had an idea that somebody should do something about this, that families needed to have this all-important "conversation" before it was too late. She decided to take action but couldn't get the domain "conversation.com." She was smart though and turned her idea into **The Conversation Project**. She *could* get that .com.

Now if you go to that site, you'll see templates and pre-prepared questions so next time you're around the dinner table with family, everyone can talk about important end-of-life health and financial issues to ensure matters will be handled according to the parents' wishes.

Please note: reserving a URL does not mean you've trademarked or patented your idea. To start that process, contact an intellectual property attorney or check the database of www.uspto.gov to see if your idea's name conflicts with an already existing business.

Reserving a URL is just the first step to developing a profitable online presence. You still need to develop useful, strategically selected content for your website that brings you up high in search engines and in the minds of your ideal customers so people can find you online.

A participant in one of my programs said, "I'm guessing that if you already have a patented product or trade-marked idea, it's not as important to get the URL?"

"Wrong!" I told him. "If you don't have your idea's related URL, you don't own your financial future."

Why do I say that? Remember, when people are first introduced to your idea, chances are they'll head to the web to find out more. Just because you have the patent or trademark, doesn't mean you own that URL. If someone else has the domain with YOUR idea's name, potential customers will go to THEIR website and may not find you. You may not even come up on the first page of search.

I learned the importance of getting an idea's URL the moment you create a one-of-a-kind name for it ... the hard way.

When I came up with the phrase Tongue Fu! ® almost 20 years ago, I went through the lengthy legal process of getting it trade-marked. However, this was before laptops, cell-phones and digital devices had become ubiquitous. Hard to believe, but my trademark attorney and I did not even discuss if I had also reserved the Tongue Fu! ® URL. (Remember, this was two decades ago.)

I used my name on my website for my speaking business and books – www.samhorn.com – and thought that was sufficient.

How naïve. Neither of us predicted back then how the internet would permeate every aspect of our personal and professional lives – and how my young sons would someday spend hours Tweeting and texting friends halfway around the world without even thinking about it. By the time I realized how crucial it was to have the Tongue Fu! ® domain name, it was too late; someone else had claimed it and was using it. Guess who? A porn company. Yikes.

I didn't think there was anything I could do. I lost hundreds of thousands of dollars over the years because people would enter www.TongueFu.com and instead of finding *my* book, corporate seminars, conference keynotes, and certification training; they were subjected to hard-core porn.

Who knows how many meeting planners, readers and potential clients innocently searched for my site – and abandoned their efforts to work with me once they opened that lurid homepage?

There is a happy ending to this story.

Victoria Stein, JD., a talented attorney and certified Tongue Fu! ® trainer, located the site owner and sent them a cease and desist letter explaining our trademark and that they were in violation of it. Thank heaven, and thanks to Victoria, they ceased and desisted.

As you can imagine, it was more complicated than that – but the good news is, thanks to a resourceful and relentless Victoria, I now own www.TongueFu.com and have learned my lesson. I now quickly reserve any and all domain sites ($12.95 is the deal of the century to reserve a potential e-commerce gold mine) as soon as I generate any idea that has commercial potential.

A program participant asked, "Sam, when I'm reserving my domain name, I know I should get .com – should I also get the .net, .org, .info etc.?"

Great question. It depends on whether you're going to wrap an entire business around your idea. Obviously, if this is a multi-million-dollar idea, it makes sense to invest an additional $18 or so (GoDaddy often gives discounts for these add-on domain names) to safeguard your idea.

This is a tiny amount of money to protect your URL and prevent the risk of others siphoning off business because they swoop in and grab the .net, .org. and info designations.

On the other hand, as mentioned, studies say 67% of people *automatically* enter .com out of habit – even if they are looking at marketing material that clearly says .info, .net or .org.

If you coin a promising name; but aren't yet sure to what extent you're going to use it, I think it's safe to just reserve the .com. If you test-market the idea and decide to pursue it; it's wise to comprehensively protect that domain by buying all the different extensions. And if your brand name, business, service or product can be spelled more than one way (or if it's commonly misspelled), be sure to register the "other" spellings.

On the other hand, if you CAN'T get the URL for something you've thought up, keep brainstorming until you come up with an option where you can get the .com.

A client asked, "Can I own more than one domain name?" The answer to that is an emphatic YES!

In fact, I have colleagues who are online landlords. They are the e-commerce equivalent of real estate investors. They have seen the future and the future is on the world wide web. They feel purchasing and parking viable domain names is relatively cheap but has huge potential pay-offs so they are quick to reserve any and all domain names of potentially viable ideas.

A client told me, "Sam, I'm so discouraged. Every time I come up with a great idea, the domain is already taken. Are there any good domain names left?"

Another good question. Did you know that more than 100 million domain names have already been registered? Thankfully, the techniques in this book can help you create brand new words to increase the likelihood you'll be able to get their domain. If you're still having a hard time getting a URL that's related to your idea, you might want to check out www.bustaname.com.

Enter your idea's core words into the BustaName system and it will brainstorm it for you by adding certain prefixes or suffixes, offering hyphenated versions and plural nouns, dropping the last vowel, and creating 2- or 3-word combinations. They provide a short video tutorial to help you get the most out of your search.

Another option is DomainTools.com (formerly WhoIs.sc). This site not only tells you if the site is taken, it looks up the history of the domain name to see if it was registered in the past, who currently owns it, where it's hosted and who it's hosted with. It's worth a try.

This is by no means a comprehensive guide to securing an idea's domain names. That's a whole book in itself. You might want to read Rob Frohwein's *Idiot's Guide to Patents, Trademarks and Copyrights* as it is a comprehensive guide that answers questions in a reader-friendly style.

Questions to Ask – Actions to Take

1. Have you already secured your idea's URL? If so, good for you. If not, jump online NOW and reserve a URL associated with it so you can capitalize on e-commerce.
2. Have you been unable to get a URL associated with your idea? Use the techniques in this chapter to brainstorm different versions of your idea so you can build a website with a URL that will bring you and your idea up in search so you can "own" your idea in the public's mind.

CHAPTER 19
Merchandise Ideas by Turning Them into Images and Icons

*"Sometimes you have to show people what they need before they know what they want." – **Steve Jobs***

Steve Jobs was right.

Concepts can be tough to grasp if they're intellectual only.

However, if you turn your concept into something concrete, your ideal customers are more likely to "get the picture." They may even say, "I see now."

The dramatic power of turning your idea into an appealing and universally identifiable image was demonstrated by a story long-time friend Marilynn Mobley, SVP for Edelman, told me.

She said a startling study was done with preschoolers. Researchers asked these kids what sounds barn-yard animals make.

For example, "What sound do sheep make?" "Baa."

"What sound do cows make?" "Moo."

"What sound do ducks make?"

The kids said, *"AFLAC!"*

Wow. Talk about a brand owning mindshare.

You may be thinking, "Okay, so the kids think ducks say AFLAC. What's that got to do with me generating a marketable, moneymaking idea?"

Here's the deal. AFLAC, the huge insurance giant, had a problem. Their name was nonsensical. And when you don't know what a company's name means, why would you do business with it? Why would you trust them with your money and give them responsibility for something as important as your life insurance policy when the name makes "no sense."

So, AFLAC wanted to turn their name into something people related to and liked. Their brilliant advertising team asked themselves, "What does AFLAC sound like, look like in the real world?"

Well, with a little stretch, it looks and sounds like a duck who quacks. This was the genesis of the ads featuring a lovable duck quacking "Aflac." Now, instead of furrowing their eyebrows and going "Huh?" when people hear or see the word AFLAC, they affectionately associate it with the insurance giant.

Another insurance conglomerate used the same principle with similar success.

Would you buy life insurance from Government Employees Insurance Company? Probably not, because you would assume they served government employees only. But then, GEICO "opened up" to the public and no longer exclusively served federal employees. They weren't as successful as anticipated because their name, a string of meaningless letters, couldn't compete with the more well-known brands of State Farm, AllState, Nationwide, etc.

So, GEICO did their version of what AFLAC did. What does a GEICO look like or sound like in the real world? Well that word sounds kind of like "gecko," those cute little lizards you find in Hawaii and the tropics. So, the friendly gecko became the visual icon and "spokesperson" (spokes-lizard?) for GEICO.

IDEApreneur

If you're thinking, "I'm still not sure how that applies to me." Well, AFLAC and GEICO went from being rather obscure insurance agencies to dramatically increasing their marketshare. They've become hugely profitable in the last few years – thanks to their brilliant decisions to turn their unappealing names into something people recognize, smile at and want to do business with. Instead of being perceived as huge anonymous companies with no "soul," customers now picture the amusing visual icons which elicit affection (a warm emotion) and customers are more favorably predisposed to entrust them with their policy.

So, what's your idea? Do you have a way of describing it so people see what you're *saying*? Does the name for your idea mean something only to you – but not to anyone else? If your idea's name or title is a nonsensical string of letters that don't resemble anything in real life, it will be hard for people to relate to you.

If people read or hear your slogan and it doesn't produce an image in their mind, it means they're not visually grasping it. And if they're not imprinting your idea, how can they remember it and recommend you to a decision-maker? What's worse, many people have adverse reactions to strange-sounding names. If they're alienated by your name, they may avoid you, your company or product altogether.

Follow the example of AFLAC and GEICO and fast-forward your idea's acceptance by giving it a visual name that conjures up an appealing image in people's mind. Connect your abstract or intellectual concept to something in the concrete world people can see, touch, feel, smell or taste.

All of a sudden, something obscure becomes clear. Something confounding will make sense. Instead of going "What?!" people will almost involuntarily say, "Oh, I see now" or "I get it now." And when *they* get it, chances are more likely *you'll* get it. You'll get their favorable attention, their curiosity, their account, business or money.

For example, a company wanted to introduce a new glue but knew it was going to be tough competing with Super Glue, the runaway top brand that had cornered the market.

If they had just called their product something like "Neil's Glue," they would have had a hard time attracting customers. Instead, (and I don't know their creative team so I'm projecting), they asked themselves, "What are the attributes of our glue? Well, it's really, really strong. What's something in the real world that's known for being really, really strong? How about gorillas?

That'd work. **Gorilla Glue.**

That name is eye-catching and ear-catching. It AFLACs their product by visually imprinting its characteristic of being strong, yet their ads feature a smiling gorilla (you don't want images that scare away customers) that pops off the page. Best of all, bottles of Gorilla Glue are popping off the shelves because people gravitate toward this idea-image and are motivated to buy it.

This displays another beauty of the AFLAC Technique. Giving your idea a visual name or icon moves people from a logical "left brain" frame of mind to an emotional "right brain" frame of mind. People make buying decisions more often from their "feeling" right brain instead of their "factual" left brain – which is why representing your idea with an image helps sell your product.

Colleague Allan Stam used this idea to come up with a memorable marketing slogan for his trade show business. Allan was competing with dozens of other consultants who help companies increase sales at their exhibition booths. What to call his services? *Take The Booth By the Horns.*

Allan then AFLAC'd his idea by developing plastic pens with a "hook 'em horns" shape at the end to reinforce his marketing slogan. He distributed these "Take the Booth by the Horns" pens which featured his contact information (they only cost pennies apiece) at his next trade fair. He said attendees were actually seeking him out to request a pen.

Furthermore, in the months ahead, every time people used that pen they were reminded of Allan's company and his website information was right there, ready to be accessed. What a great example of ongoing visual name recognition and positive branding that leads to increased sales.

Questions to Ask – Actions to Take

1. Does your idea have a nonsensical name people don't understand? Does it create confusion and you have to keep explaining it but it still doesn't make sense to them? Explain.
2. Ask yourself, "What does my idea look or sound like in the real world? How can I associate it with something people can picture in their mind's eye? How can I give my concept a visual icon or concrete image so they can *see* what I'm saying and what I mean?

CHAPTER 20
Become a Topic Expert Who Gets Paid to Speak

"I have the world's best job. I get paid to hang out in my imagination all day." – **Stephen King**

I AGREE with Stephen King. It is indeed a privilege and a pleasure to be able to make your living from your imagination.

I have had the distinct honor of being in the "idea" business for 25+ years. I have thoroughly enjoyed making a good living from my mind. I love creating proprietary intellectual capital and turning that into a rewarding and profitable career on the page, on the stage and online.

After every presentation, at least a couple people come up to say, "I want to do what you do. How can I get paid to speak?"

If you'd like to get paid to speak on your ideas, your next step after reading this book is to visit www.NSAspeaker.org for information about their local chapters and national conferences.

I was involved in NSA for 25 years and learned a lot from such masters as Glenna Salsbury, Lou Hecklar and Jeanne Robertson. There's no better way to fast-track your career than learning from the best in the business and I vouch for the benefits of being involved in NSA.

If your primary goals are to establish yourself as a topic expert, attract clients, gain name recognition and visibility, drive sales for your business or book, and share your idea (s) with others, then you're in the right place. Not only is it possible for you to get paid to speak, you could be making money from public seminars within the next 3-4 months – for hardly a dime out of your pocket.

I'm speaking from experience (so to speak) as this is the approach I used to launch my career as a professional speaker.

In the late 1970's, I was reading the *Washington Post* and noticed that the word "concentration" was used six times on the front page of the sports section.

Tennis player Chris Evert claimed her ability to concentrate – despite the noisy planes flying overhead – was why she'd been able to win the U.S. Open.

A golfer blamed the clicking cameras of nearby photographers for why he'd become distracted and blown a short putt on a sudden death play-off hole.

A baseball team that had been leading their division lost their last 7 games and didn't make the playoffs. In a press conference, their dejected manager said, "We got ahead of ourselves and started thinking about who we'd face in the playoffs instead of focusing on winning today's game."

I was intrigued. I thought, "Concentration is something we all wish we could do better. And yet no one ever teaches us how to do it. We're taught how to spell, write, do math, but no one ever.

teaches us how to pay attention when we want or need to. I've never seen any books on this topic. I've never heard anyone speak on it."

My idea was to put together a public workshop on "How to Concentrate." I thought it was something people wanted to do better and they would pay to have someone teach them and their employees (and kids!) how to concentrate.

I knew from experience that concentration was a skill that could be learned. It isn't this mysterious ability you either have or don't have. It can be *taught*.

I'd played competitive tennis for my high school and college, and had the privilege of working with Rod Laver (who twice won the Grand Slam of Tennis) on Hilton Head Island, SC.

Rocket was compact and rather short for a tennis player (5'7); but he made up for it with his work ethic, championship mentality, and ability to concentrate – no matter what. He learned to concentrate in the hot Australian sun with thousands of hours of drills on the practice court. He taught me that the ability to focus was as important, if not more important, than athletic ability.

As he said, "The top twenty players on the tour have similar fitness and athletic skill. It is their will to win, their ability not to get distracted by doubts, by the crowd, by the pressure that determines who walks away with the trophy."

I couldn't get this idea of offering a public workshop on the topic of concentration out of my head. And as discussed earlier, that's a sure sign an idea has value and deserves to be pursued.

So, I started researching the topic and interviewing people. I interviewed athletes, artists, executives, entrepreneurs, taxi drivers, tax preparers and teachers, and asked questions delving into every aspect of the subject. Sample questions included:

- What's your definition of concentration?
- Did anyone ever teach you how to concentrate (a parent, coach, teacher)? If so, put me in the scene and re-enact it? What did they tell you to do? What did they tell you not to do?
- When is a time you concentrated well? (Reading a book and getting lost in the story? Rushing to meet a tight deadline? Immersed in a hobby you love? Describe what happened. What *contributed* to you being able to concentrate in that situation?)
- Would you say you're good at concentrating? Why or why not?
- What are two specific things you do to focus and maintain your attention?
- What compromises your ability to concentrate? What causes you to lose your focus?
- Who is someone you think is good at concentrating – no matter what? A famous athlete or actor? Your boss? A surgeon? A musician or magician? Why did you pick him/her?
- If you would like to learn one thing about concentration, what would that be?
- What's one piece of advice you would give to someone who wanted to learn how to concentrate better?

I accumulated the best-practice tips culled from these interviews and added my own insights – and turned them into a step-by-step methodology people could use to concentrate better – anytime, anywhere and on anything.

I approached Open University (the precursor to Learning Annex, a popular adult education program open to the public) and pitched my course on **Concentration.**

Sandy Bremer, the owner, agreed to offer it. At the end of my first three-hour workshop, 16 people came up afterwards and asked if I'd speak for their organization or association. That one evening launched my speaking career.

When I moved to Hawaii in the early 80's, I approached Dr. Ray Oshiro of University of Hawaii's Continuing Education department and pitched my **Concentration** course to him.

He liked the description and offered it as a half day workshop on a Saturday morning. Thirty five people signed up. At the end of the session, even more participants walked up to ask if I'd speak for their convention or company. Would I?! That one session jump-started my business in my new home state.

I have been speaking professionally ever since – getting paid well to do work I love that matters. I am grateful to Sandy of Open U and Ray of UH, for helping to launch such a satisfying career.

The following steps are the same ones I took to get my foot in the door with public speaking engagements around the country.

I'm partial. I think this is one of the quickest ways to catapult your speaking career.

Why? They get you in front of a diverse audience – a cross-section of people who are active in different professions, clubs and companies – who have a first-hand opportunity to experience you in action. If you do a quality job, they often choose to become a client and they often turn into word-of-mouth ambassadors who promote you and your work to their colleagues.

To share everything, I've learned in the past 25 years about how to become a paid professional speaker would take a whole book. For now, I've distilled my best-practice tips on how to get paid to speak on your idea into the following steps. They can help you turn your value-adding idea into a lucrative, rewarding speaking career if you follow up on them.

1. Identify the most successful adult education-lifelong learning program in your area.

This could be a private organization like the Boston Center for Adult Education which is housed at an elegant mansion near Commonwealth Ave, or in school classrooms at University of San Francisco's College of Extended Learning or Foothill College's Community Learning Center. (Side note: From the 1970's to 2010, there was a version of Learning Annex, Discover U, First Class and Open U. in every major city. Many of them have either gone out of business, changed their business model, feature celebrities only as teachers, or have switched to online courses.)

If there is no thriving adult education program in your area, find out which of the service clubs – Rotary, Exchange, Lions, Kiwanis – has members of your target demographic.

If your idea would appeal to entrepreneurs and executives, then you might want to find out which club meets downtown and has the most active membership of businessmen and women.

If your idea is more relevant to retirees, then you might want to find a club with a lot of boomers who are about to retire and who have already retired.

Also, look up the local chapters of the professional association that is related to your idea and topic. There are professional associations for veterinarians, engineers, Mars enthusiasts, toy collectors, physical therapists, and Barbershop singers. And almost all of them have local meetings, statewide conferences and national conventions. And almost all of them are looking for quality speakers who could thrill their members with relevant insights/expertise.

2. Go online to research the organization. How often do they meet and/or offer classes? Where? What's the profile of their membership? What types of speakers do they feature? What types of topics or classes have been offered recently? Do they have a proposal form or submission policy online? Do they have a local, state and national convention? What is the phone number and name of the program chair or coordinator?

3. Determine what topics they have NOT offered in your area of expertise. This is very important. Most of these organizations are loyal to their current instructors and do not want to repeat topics given recently. If you pitch a session similar to something already in their catalogue or that they have addressed in a recent meeting, they will say NO THANKS, regardless of your qualifications, the value of your idea or how great a description you write.

4. Craft an intriguing description of your proposed presentation/workshop on your letterhead **in the exact same format and length used by this organization**. *This is crucial.* If their descriptions are 100 words long, your description needs to be 100 words long. If they feature mostly bullet points of benefits, your description better feature bullet points. If their instructor bios are only two sentences long, trim your bio into two sentences that highlight your most impressive credentials.

5. Fill out *their* RFP or submission form – but DO NOT SUBMIT IT YET. Be sure your description doesn't duplicate something they're already offering or have recently featured.

6. Have your one-page description ready AND their filled-out form on your desk … and then call the program coordinator. If you're applying to present a program for an adult education program, *call at least 2 weeks before the deadline.* If you're calling to volunteer to speak at a weekly or monthly service club meeting, call at least 3 months before you'd like to speak.

7. The first words out of your mouth are, "Bill (or Susan), I know you're busy, and may I have two minutes of your time?" These decision-makers are usually quite busy so they will probably say, "Keep it brief" and it's up to you to have crafted a concise, compelling, commercially viable "pitch" that favorably impresses them in those 2 minutes.

8. If you have 6 degrees of separation, use them. Say, "Katie Brenham has presented programs for you for the past couple of years and rec-

ommended I get in touch with you." Or "Max Krell spoke for you a few months ago, and thought my topic might be of interest to your members."

9. Next, say, "I've had a chance to review your course catalogue and would like to propose a program that would add value for your customers – and that doesn't duplicate any of your current programs."
Or you can say, "Max told me your members really appreciated his talk on stress management, and they might be interested in the new research that shows startling ways to reduce it."

These are magic words as they let the decision-maker know you've done your homework and are pitching something new. Just as stores change their inventory every 6 weeks so their merchandise is new (instead of same old, same old), these organizations want to feature new sessions so returning members and customers see something "fresh" they want to sign up for.

10. When they ask for your credentials or ask, "What's your background?" be sure to focus on names and numbers. Instead of making a vague claim such as "I'm a consultant on this topic" or a sweeping generalization such as "I've researched this topic," be specific. "I've consulted on this topic for 5 years with such clients as Intel and Amgen." or "I'm a physician at Kaiser in internal medicine and have written and presented a white paper on this at our annual meeting."

11. The program coordinator will probably say something like, "Send me the submission form and I'll look it over," at which point you say, "I'll be glad to mail that submission form to you AND I have a one-page course description and bio right in front of me that is in the same format you use in your catalog. May I email it to you?"

In the 20 years I've been using this approach, I've never had one person say, "NO."

By the way, in the old days (3-20 years ago), I would ask, "Is it okay if I FAX this one-page description and bio to you?"

Why did I offer to *fax* my one-pager? Because it would be on their desk seconds later, in the exact same format/length they use. It made it very easy for them to say YES because they could insert it right into their catalogue or marketing materials. What's not to like??

Why not just mail their RFP or standard submission form on its own? Because it will probably get tossed in the file with all the other proposed courses. The decision-maker will look at a couple weeks later with all the dozens of other proposals. Not only will you be out of sight, out of mind, your idea could get lost in that crowd.

If you email or fax your one-pager, they have a compelling description of a program they HAVEN'T already offered that would appeal to their members and customers ... seconds after they've just had a delightful conversation with an impressively prepared, sensitive professional who did their homework.

Even if the program coordinator says they're not interested for some reason, ask if you can still email your proposal so they can keep it on file for the future, just in case. Who knows, they may come across it a few months later and decide it would be the perfect addition to their offerings. This is exactly what happened with Foothill College. They didn't think one of the programs I would be offering for women leaders would get a large enough sign-up to offer from their membership; but two months later the program coordinator called to ask if I'd be interested in speaking for an AAUW (American Association of University Women) meeting held in Silicon Valley. Not only did I end up speaking for that event, two female executives from Hewlett-Packard were at that session and asked me to bring the program into their organization.

12. If the program coordinator says "Yes," (which hopefully they will since you made it easy for them to do so), be sure to take entrepreneur-

ial responsibility for marketing the course. Create your own one-page flyer on your letterhead with the description of the course, your bio, and testimonials, along with a registration link from the sponsoring organization.

The Adult Ed organization will promote your program to its mailing list and in its catalog, but you want to do everything you can to bring this program to the attention of as many people as possible. Purposely attend a variety of professional meetings (i.e., Chamber of Commerce, EWomen Network, ATD, SHRM) in your area in the six weeks before your program. When people request your card or ask what you do, hand them this flyer instead of your card. This is a conversation-starter and gives you a chance to talk up your program and invite them to attend.

If you're speaking for a Rotary, Kiwanis, Exchange or Lions Club, ask their policy about guests. Many of these organizations welcome guests (who pay a slightly higher fee for the lunch or dinner program) because they're always recruiting and trying to grow their clubs.

13. In addition to prominently featuring your Adult Ed program or club presentation on your website, in your newsletter and social media posts, build buzz for your program by submitting a 150 - 300-word article (with a photo) to your local business journal, women's newspaper, health/fitness magazine and association newsletter.

The free periodicals you find in the lobby of Safeway, Publix, and Whole Food or at the library usually welcome freelance articles that offer useful tips. This is a good way to put you and your idea, business, and program on the mental map of residents in the area. (More specific tips on this in Chapter 23).

14. A skeptical Hall of Fame speaker who knows how much I normally get paid for a presentation, "Sam, why do you still speak for service clubs, adult education organizations and local association meetings? It's pro bono, or you only make a fraction of your normal fee. I don't get it."

I smiled and told him, "How much would I pay to have a photo of my book cover, a compelling description of my topic, and a bio with my credentials in front of thousands of my ideal customers in my area or millions of people across the country?"

How much would I pay for SOMEONE ELSE to sponsor public seminars for me and to pay ALL the overhead, coordinate ALL the logistics, handle ALL the registrations - so all I have to do is show up and deliver a quality program that produces real-world results and exceeds?

How much would I pay for NOT having to incur expenses for a meeting room, provide my own AV, cover out-of-pocket marketing costs, and worry about how many people will sign up and whether I will make back my overhead?

"How much would I pay to have a public forum where I can invite decision-makers who are thinking of hiring me so they have a no-risk opportunity to see me in action and make up their minds about whether I'm right for their group?

How much would I pay for opportunities to stay in front of my target market three times a year so I can maintain positive name and face recognition on an ongoing basis? These brochures are often distributed to hundreds of thousands of people – and thousands more check the websites to "browse" the offerings. This means millions of people I never would have met otherwise now know about my idea, book, topic, and that I speak, write and consult on this issue.

Not only do I NOT have to fund all the above and incur worry and risk, all the above is FREE. This long-time speaker said, "But isn't it true these classes or club meetings usually draw a few dozen people? Your normal audience usually has several hundred or several thousand people."

"That's true, but how many people SAW that write-up of my workshop in that course catalog which is distributed to their mailing list? They may not sign up for the workshop, but they may be in a bookstore a few weeks later, see my book and be motivated to buy it because they remember reading that nice review in the BCAE brochure. They may not be in town to attend the seminar, but they may be in charge of their employee orientation later that year and decide my topic would be perfect for their event.

There's a saying in our industry, "The more you speak, the more you speak."

That may look trite; however, it's actually quite profound.

When you're trying to get traction for your idea, visibility is everything. You have to get your idea out of inertia and introduce it to people who are in a position to try it and buy it, to tell other people about it and to become a fan of it and an advocate for it.

You've got to create momentum, and that doesn't happen sitting at home waiting for someone to discover you. Presenting public seminars, speaking for service clubs, or presenting for associations that have members in your target demographic is a pro-active way to kick-start your ideas' visibility and your name recognition as a topic expert and an IDEApreneur.

Remember, you can use these public seminars as no-risk opportunities for decision-makers to see you in action. Is State Farm thinking of hiring you but they're on the fence? Ask the Training Director or one of their staff members to attend your service club program as your guest. Use that program as a forum to invite media so they can film a "remote" segment and interview attendees about a news-making topic to produce an interesting segment.

Recognize that a cross-section of individuals attend these programs. If a couple dozen people are in the room, you now have people in twenty companies in your area who know about your speaking – and each of those individuals is probably active in other clubs or associations. If you do an excellent job, you have thrown your "speaking stone into the pond" and the ripple effect will start spreading word of mouth about you.

Please note: ALWAYS ACT IN INTEGRITY AND DO NOT PITCH FROM THE PLATFORM. I believe we have a contract with every audience and that is to provide relevant, tangible, inspiring insights they can use to produce real-world results. If you do that, people will Socratically decide they want to know more about you, whether that's to work with you or buy your products. Do not use *their* time to sell from the stage. That is annoying, offensive, will alienate most people, and will undermine our reputation because it will make other meeting planners reluctant to book you lest you do it to *their* audience.

At the end of the program, you can let people know you would be happy to talk with them at your book-signing, booth, or at the back of the room about the different products and services you have available.

15. A major key to monetizing your idea and intellectual capital can be summed up in one word -- database. Many e-commerce experts feel 10,000 names in your database is the magic number. That's enough critical mass to play the percentages so when you offer a new product or program, there will be enough purchases to produce ongoing income.

So, at every public presentation, you might want to have a drawing to give away a door prize (one of your products or a gift certificate towards your services?) and to collect business cards and/or email addresses to add to your database. Ask yourself, "What could I offer as a give-away that people would value?" A free report? A complementary 30-minute coaching session?

Mailing lists require opt-in, so be sure to clarify that people who enter the drawing or giveaway will have their name added to your mailing list and get written permission.

16. John Kotter of Harvard says, "Do you know the #1 prerequisite to change? A sense of urgency." You might want to offer on-site discount on your back-of-the-room products to provide a sense of urgency so people have incentive to buy something at the end of the session ... but make it *genuine*. Perhaps you could bundle your products and offer a volume discount or a specially priced package of learning resources so people can take them back to their office and set up a lending library for fellow employees so even more people can benefit from your ideas.

We've all seen cheesy "Just for the first ten people ..." "I NEVER do this, but for you ..." It's legit to offer an on-site discount as long as they don't then go online and see you offering the same discount or lower prices than promised.

17. The good news is, the decision-makers at these Adult Ed programs "talk to each other" and share resources with others in their network. So, if you do a good job at Boston Center for Adult Education, you then have your foot in the door of similar programs across the United States. When you call the program coordinator in a new city, start with "This program was well-received at (what other association, club or Adult Ed organization?). We had (how many people?) register and (the name of the program coordinator) said the evaluations were (what ranking?)"

One of the goals of growing your idea's success is to "take it national or international." That's why, once you have spoken for several organizations in your area, you want to start reaching out to similar organization in other areas around the country.

If you want your idea to go viral, I suggest you schedule as many presentations as you can in a "tight time window" to build critical mass so people think, "I see you EVERYWHERE!"

Ideas, books and issues go viral when there is a flurry of national or international online posts, likes, forwards. Identify 10 major cities (i.e.,

IDEApreneur

New York, Boston, Washington DC, Chicago, Atlanta, Houston, Denver, Seattle, San Francisco, Los Angeles) and coordinate a cross country tour to accelerate visibility and media coverage in large cities over a 3-week time period.

18. Whatever you do, TEACH THE COURSE AND GIVE A QUALITY PRESENTATION, no matter how many people are in the room. Never cancel a course (even if there are only a handful of registrations) as this will close this pipeline forever. You want to honor your commitment to the organization and to whoever cared enough to show up. I've heard some professional speakers say, "It's not 'worth' teaching a class for under ten people. I disagree. Everyone counts. I don't believe in measuring our success by numbers. If six people show up, then we do our best to make sure this is the best workshop they've ever attended so they feel they got full value. That is how you build a reputation for integrity. That's how you establish yourself as a professional that program coordinators and meeting planners can trust to deliver results for their customers and members. It's just how you want to be in the world.

Two of my favorite all-time book-signings had less than a dozen people show up. One I had booked months in advance at the Borders at South Coast Mall in Southern California without realizing it was the night of the … Academy Awards.

The CRC (Community Relations Coordinator) called the week before to ask if I wanted to cancel since she wasn't sure anyone would attend. I assured her I wanted to go ahead with it. That evening a single mother drove an hour and a half to get there. She told me she had saved her grocery money to pay for a babysitter and that she "had" to come meet me in person because my book (*What's Holding You Back?*) had been a lifesaver for her. Was it worth holding that booksigning/seminar? You bet it was.

The other was at an independent bookstore in San Francisco. A family of three arrived early with a dog-eared, heavily underlined copy of *Take the Bully by the Horns*. This mother, father, and their 13-year-old daughter said it had been their "bible" in dealing with some mean girls at school. The young girl, Katherine, was bright and an absolute delight. I encouraged her to write about her experiences. We're still in touch several years later. She emailed me just recently to tell me that one of her articles was published in *Stone Soup*, a magazine for young writers.

Was it worth holding that book-signing/seminar for a handful of people? An emphatic and heartfelt yes.

19. Are you thinking, "Okay, all this makes sense, but it looks like most of these presentations are done for free or for not much money. I need and want to monetize my idea and generate revenue from speaking. How do I do that?"

First things first. Use this system to get a number of successful speaking engagements under your belt and to establish a reputation as someone meeting planners can trust to deliver results.

Then, use these steps to go from free to fee – and to start negotiating more equitable quid pro quo trades and income for speaking.

a. In your conversation with the meeting planner, ask, "What's your budget for speakers?"
If they say, "Oh, we don't pay our speakers" or "This is pro bono," then here's what you say.

"I'd like to speak for you and my normal fee for a presentation like this is $_____. Let's get creative to see how we can make this happen."

b. Why is it important to say, "My normal fee is..." Because if people come up to the meeting planner afterwards and say, "Wow, Steve was great, how much did he charge?" and the meeting planner says, "He spoke for free" then your reputation is that you speak for free.

IDEApreneur

If you say, "Well, my normal fee is $1500," then the meeting planner will say, "Well, his normal fee is $1500, but he agreed to speak for us in trade for … "

c. Here are some of the "trades" you could consider exchanging for your normal fee.

- A professional video and audio recording of the presentation (that you can sell, share on YouTube or post on your website).
- A booth at their local, state convention or annual meeting where you can sell your products.
- A quarter or half page ad in their monthly newsletter for one to 12 months, (depending on the fair market value of your fee) to advertise your business, events and services.
- A recommendation (if you do a good job) to their national or international convention chair. o An opportunity to offer a longer, for fee, workshop for members that they promote.
- An agreement to do a podcast, submit a blog or be interviewed for a feature in their national magazine or on their website.
- Ten social media posts (on Facebook, Twitter, LinkedIn) to their following in the 2 weeks preceding and following the program.
- An agreement to reduce your fee on a ONE-TIME BASIS if they understand that when they ask you back in the future - or recommend you to others - it will be at your full fee.

e. Most meeting planners are more than willing to get creative and make this a win for you – if you ask graciously and professionally. They will also take you more seriously and will tend to value what you do for them. Instead of just being "another weekly or monthly speaker" – one of many over the years – you will stand out as a pro who negotiated an equitable agreement and delivered on your end of it – which will motivate them to deliver on theirs.

Are you thinking, "Okay, this seems like a good plan. But I'm not comfortable presenting in public." Or, "I love to speak, but I still get nervous because I haven't done it very much."

Then, your next step is https://www.toastmasters.org/, a 90-year-old organization that has helped millions (really) of people around the globe improve their speaking skills. No matter where you live and work, there is probably a chapter nearby.

My grandfather, George Reed, was actually International President of this organization in 1951, and I've had the privilege of speaking at their annual convention and being a judge at their local competitions. It is an excellent way to develop your speaking skills so you can confidently and compellingly communicate your idea so others get it and want it. It's a worthwhile investment in your idea's success and in your success as an IDEApreneur.

Questions to Ask – Actions to Take

1. Do you enjoy speaking in public? Do you do it often? Describe a time you spoke in front of a group and audience members found it intriguing and useful.
2. Are you already presenting programs on your idea? If so, how can you use these techniques to schedule more engagements? If not, how can you use these techniques to start speaking at your local service club, association meeting or adult education center? 3. Are you already getting paid to speak? If so, good for you. If not, how are you going to use these techniques to negotiate for trades so you're being valued for what you're delivering and so you start receiving compensation "in trade" for presenting on your idea?

CHAPTER 21
Get Paid to Consult /Coach on Your Idea

"To do what you love and feel that it matters, how could anything be more fun? – **Katherine Graham** *of the Washington Post*

I TELL YOU what could be more fun. To do what you love, feel that it matters, and **get paid for it**.

If you're a successful IDEApreneur, people will want to "pick your brain."

It's important to set up policies and boundaries so you can "give back" and support others but your generous spirit doesn't get taken advantage of.

I'll always remember a consulting client, a former president of a large association, who asked for help with this issue. She gets calls and emails all the time from people who want to "buy her a cup of coffee" or "take her to lunch" so they can ask for her advice.

She is an incredibly gracious person so she often spends a half hour or more answering their questions on the phone or sending thoughtfully-prepared emails. If they live in her area, she usually agrees to meet with them. They ask lots of questions, gets thousands of dollars of free advice and then pick up the tab for the cup of coffee. That is *not* quid pro quo.

She told me, "When I was President, I knew this 'came with the territory,' so I was glad to do it. After a year of traveling 300 days last year, around the world, on behalf of the association, I now need to focus on making money and this is taking up way too much of my time.

"I want to support people in my industry and I don't want to come across as a snob, but these people drain my energy, run with my recommendations, and make a lot of money from my contacts and all I get out of it is a thank you card ... maybe."

I told her, "As Jack Canfield says, 'People treat us the way we teach them to treat us.'

"Most people will not volunteer to pay you for advice unless you clarify up front that you do this for a living. Some people are clueless and for others, it might not occur to them that their "Just one question?" email or "cup of coffee invitation" is one of *dozens* you receive every single week from other people who also want your wisdom."

I continued, "It took you years to accumulate this wisdom and it is fair for you to get compensated for contributing your experience and expertise. They're going to profit from your advice so it's fair that they compensate you for giving them ideas that translate into cash."

She said, "Sam, I know that's true in theory. In practice, it's hard for me to bring up the issue of money because most of them seem to think I should be glad to mentor them since I'm kind of known for that."

"I understand that's been your reputation in the past, *and* it's time to set and enforce your boundaries so people respect your expertise. People can't read your mind. It's up to YOU to graciously and firmly let them know your policy about this so they know the ground-rules."

Please note: I absolutely believe in giving back to our professional community. I think it's important for us to support individuals who are starting out in their careers.

In balance.

I also know – from experience – that **"our strength taken to an extreme becomes our weakness."**

Kindness and generosity are wonderful qualities – however if we continue to be kind and generous to people who are taking advantage of our kindness and generosity, then those qualities become our Achilles Heel.

A commitment to help others is a marvelous characteristic – but if we let people take, take, take while we continue to give, give, give; it is only a matter of time before we burn out.

As Ann Landers said, "People can't walk all over you if you don't lie down."

By all means, continue to share your wisdom in an equitable way. Just remember, it's *your* responsibility to make sure it stays a win-win. The following policy can help you do that.

A Policy for Charging for Your Mind and Time (Which is Consulting)

1. From now on, when people call or email with a "quick question" or an invitation to get together for a cup of coffee because they want to pick your brain, **formalize the process** by saying, "I've got time available later this week (or next week). You're welcome to schedule a complementary 15-minute appointment to discuss this."

This does several things. It lets them know you're busy and that **time with you needs to be scheduled**. If you pick up the phone or return the call to give advice, guess what happens? You have set a precedent of instant, around-the-clock access. They'll respond with a follow-up question and will feel free to call or email any time they want to ask for your advice.

If you answer their question in a quick email, you have just established a dangerous norm of being at their beck and call. They will think nothing of emailing with another request because they don't perceive there's anything wrong with asking for a quick favor.

2. You say, "I consult on this issue all the time and I'll be happy to answer your question in a complementary 15- minute call. At the end of 15 minutes, if you'd like to continue brainstorming or go deeper, we can discuss my consulting rates and you can decide how you'd like to proceed."

This sets clear parameters on how much free time you'll give them. Plus, this is a win-win. They can tap into your accumulated knowledge so you are "giving back" to your peers. Yet at the same time, you are honoring your right to get paid for your expertise.

3. As the conversation nears 15 minutes, say (interrupt if necessary), "Steve, I've enjoyed our conversation and we have time for one more question." If they keep talking or beg for more time, say, "Steve, I hope this has been helpful. I've got another call coming up, so I need to wrap this up. If you're interested, I'll be glad to send you information about my consulting services."

Remember, you're not being "mean," you just mean what you say.

4. You might want to offer your consulting in time packages. For example, a half day or four hour package. A full day or eight-hour package. Or a weekend or 16-hour package.

Research shows that offering three options reduces price resistance because it gives potential clients different entry points that are in alignment with their budget. People who don't have much money can come in at the "silver" or lowest price level.

Others who always want the best or who are really serious about this and want to do a deep dive will take the "platinum" or highest-priced level. Traditionally, the majority will opt for the middle "gold" level, the mid-priced option.

5. Some consultants and coaches choose to be on a "retainer basis" for 3 months, 6 months or 12 month contracts. These types of retainer contractors are often for a certain number of hours each month – or unlimited access - via phone, Skype, Google hangouts and email. Be careful about offering "unlimited" access as you can get swamped answering emails and lengthy phone calls.

6. **You may be wondering, "How much do I charge?'** The answer to that question depends on many variables including:

- **Your proven track record of expertise and results in this field** (*New York Times* bestselling author? Scaled sales in an organization 200% in one year? Managed 600 employees? Lost 100 pounds and have kept it off for ten years? Olympic level athlete?)
- **Educational degrees or certifications** (MBA? Master Certified Coach? Ph. D?)
- **The name status of the organizations you've been associated with/ worked for** (Fortune 500? Google? National media like CBS or MSNBC? SXSW?)
- **The potential bottom-line monetary value of consult** (Will you be connecting them with investors, agents, publishers they wouldn't meet otherwise? Will you be helping them come up with a funding pitch that will land them millions?)
- **The going rate in your industry and location** (Are career coaches in your area charging $150/hour and your credentials are similar or better? Then, it would be fair for you to charge the same. Are website designers receiving $5000 to create a 10-page blog site? If so, what is their track record and do you compare favorably?)

It's also important to factor in supply and demand.

If you're starting from scratch or want to grow your coaching/consulting business, you might initially set your fees low for a certain amount of time to build your client list. Let people know this fee is for the next six months only and will be increased at the beginning of the year.

7. Payment is usually made in full at the time of scheduling the first appointment (or automatically on their credit card per month) to minimize the back-and-forth invoicing and collection. It's smart to arrange for PayPal or for credit card payments as that is the preferred method of most customers.

8. Develop an agreement letter regarding your policies and procedures. For example, clients may email up to 3 pages in advance of each appt. and you agree to study/brainstorm/strategize that submitted material *before* the consultation to prime your mental pump so you can hit the ground running.

Be sure to enforce that boundary. If a client sends their manuscript and says, "I know it's more than 3 pages, but I was hoping you could just skim it so you're familiar with it," let them know you will look at the FIRST 3 pages. Anything else will be on the clock or reviewed during your consulting time together.

Have a reschedule/cancel policy. For example, appointments can be re-scheduled with no penalty up to 48 hours in advance. If a client cancels within 48 hours of the appt, half of the fee is charged to their account (since it's assumed you held that time for them and won't be able to rebook it).

9. Start each appointment with "I've been looking forward to talking with you. What shall we focus on to make the most of our time together?"

NO chit chat or small talk about the weather. When people are paying by the hour and minute, they don't want to discuss the weather or exchange "How are you's." Jump right into business and stay focused on their priorities so they feel they're getting their money's worth.

10. **Suggest that clients record the call.** Often, when you are interviewing them about their idea or brainstorming next steps, you'll both be in that stream-of-consciousness state of flow in which you say something "just right." If they don't write this "verbal gold" down immediately, that perfect language or brilliant insight could be lost.

Furthermore, if they record the call, they can listen to it over and over and pick up things they missed the first time around. It doubles and triples the value of your consult because it delivers ongoing bottom-line value.

11. If someone wants to "talk shop" and you want to support that person, you may want to suggest a "walk/talk." I started doing this years ago because I need to exercise a lot more than I need to eat. Many IDEApreneurs work inside at their computer all day (and night.) When someone offers to take me to lunch, I let them know they're welcome to join me on my walk (with pen and paper in hand.) I get out from behind my desk and get outside to exercise - they get to ask whatever they want – we both have a thoroughly enjoyable time. Now that's a win-win.

So, are you ready to get paid to consult/coach on your ideas. These step-by-step tips can help you get started. You may also want to check out the International Coach Federation – https://www.coachfederation.org – which has chapters in most major cities around the world.

ICF hosts monthly programs and annual conventions and in person and online accreditation programs that can help you become a professional coach or consultant who makes a good living advising people in your area of expertise.

Questions to Ask – Actions to Take

- Do people ask you for free advice? Do people want to "pick your brain?" How do you feel about that? What are the pros and cons?
- Are you ready to set up some policies around sharing your valuable wisdom? What specific steps are you going to take to formalize a consulting/coaching process? Are you going to research ICF and attend a local meeting or look into certification?
- From now on, when someone asks, "Can I buy you a cup of coffee? I'd love to pick your brain." What are you going to say? How will you enforce your boundaries around this?

CHAPTER 22
Get Paid to Write on Your Idea

"I'd like to have money. And I'd like to be a good writer. I hope these two can come together." – **Dorothy Parker**

AS YOU CAN IMAGINE, it would take a whole book to explain how to crystallize, write, pitch, publish and market a quality book and blog.

Fortunately, you don't have to read a whole book to start making money from your writing.

You can start generating revenue now by writing special reports, white papers and e-books.

And the good news is, they take a fraction of the time, effort and expense required to complete an entire 200-300-page tome.

Jeffrey J. Mayer was the first person to bring this option to my attention. I had known Jeffrey for years. Our careers had somewhat paralleled each other's. We were both members of National Speakers Association, both had active careers presenting for associations and corporations, and both had books with New York publishers.

Jeffrey was famous for his book *If You Don't Have Time To Do It Right, When Will You Have Time To Do It Over?* (Great title, right? Long, but it resonates since we relate to it.) Jeffrey walked up to me after I had presented a program on how **That's Original!** for our annual convention.

He said, "Sam, why are you still suggesting people pursue the traditional publishing route?"

Puzzled, I asked, "What do you mean?"

He said, "We both know how hard it is to get a deal with a major publisher like Random House or Simon & Schuster. And even if we get a deal, it takes a minimum of 18 months for our book to hit the shelves and then it has to 'earn out' before we make any royalties from it."

"Yeah," I said, "So?"

"Last year I wrote an article for my local business journal in Chicago. The article was such a hit I got flooded with requests for permission to reprint it. After a while I got tired of sending copies out, so I thought, 'I'm going to start selling these.'

"I asked myself, "How much should I charge for this?' I had no idea, so on the spur of the moment I just arbitrarily decided…$17."

"Sam," he said, pausing for emphasis, "I sold 30,000 copies of that article for $17.

"People loved my approach to opening doors with a brilliant elevator speech. They ordered it for themselves and then ordered copies for their employees. Then, a sales manager asked me to expand it and include tips on how his team could introduce themselves over the phone, and turn their Elevator Speech into a sales call that got their foot in the door. I expanded it to thirty pages and charged $27 for it. I sold thousands more copies."

He looked at me, eyebrows raised in amazement. "And that's all with NO shipping, NO fulfillment, NO inventory, No shlepping to the post office, NO packaging.

"People just order it and download it so there's no head-ache. I never have to leave my office. I just sit in front of my computer and answer my phone and collect credit card information all day. Ka-ching. It took me a few hours to write one article and it's been producing sheer profit ever since."

Now I was incredulous. "Jeffrey, why would people pay $27 for a thirty-page report when they can go to their local bookstore and pay a third of that for a three-hundred-page book?"

"That's the point," he said. "We live in an instant gratification society. People don't want to have to get in their cars, drive to a bookstore, browse the shelves to try to find just the right book and search through dozens of chapters to find what they want.

"They want information NOW. I've condensed what they needed to know into thirty succinct, information-packed pages they can instantly download and have in their hands in seconds for a click of a button. What's not to like?

"Plus, I offer a money-back guarantee so there's no risk. If someone doesn't think it's worthwhile, they're welcome to request a refund and I promise to give them their money back. No questions asked. There's no downside. In all this time, only a handful of people have asked for a refund so this a no-brainer."

Hmmm. What Jeffrey – and many other IDEApreneurs now know – is that offering written learning resources online is a potential perpetual bonanza.

A sad addendum to the above story. Unfortunately, Jeffrey passed away a few years ago. Yet his website – www.SucceedingInBusiness.com – and his many e-books (including the original *How to Open Doors with a Brilliant Elevator Speech*) live on, proving that online information products are truly Equity Ideas that continue to generate revenue without you having to be there. Jeffrey dedicated himself to producing valuable e-books that make a difference for people and they continue to make money for his family.

I'd like to share the two most important tips I've learned on how you can produce Special Reports and e-books that provide substantive value so people WANT to buy them.

1. Write Headlines that Focus on a Problem or Pain People are Experiencing.

This is one of the most important lessons I've learned, although I've been the author equivalent of an aircraft carrier getting turned around on this one.

I've been a professional speaker – an IDEApreneur – who's earned my living from designing and delivering intellectual capital for twenty-five years. I specialize in original how-to's that help people live a more effective and satisfying personal and professional life.

And therein lies the problem (so to speak.) I focus on how-to's. How to communicate better. How to concentrate better. How to walk into a room full of strangers and turn them into friends. How to create a one-of-a-kind title. And so on.

Those are nice. But they're not urgent. Those are "higher-order" concepts people would like to achieve when they have more time, more money or when they're not quite so busy.

But for now, the only thing that has the power to really grab their attention is something that focuses on a challenge they're currently facing. See, that's more pressing. That's top of mind. That's what motivates people to stop what they're doing and pay attention and pay money – because they want to stop the pain and solve the problem.

There's no better example of this than a full-page ad that runs frequently in *USA TODAY*. I've been told these ads cost a quarter of a million dollars, so you know these ads are producing impressive payoffs for the sponsor - Fisher Investments – since they keep running them week after week.

Why are these ads so successful? Well, in my opinion because they offer a FREE report with no risk – and because they feature bullet points – ALL of which pinpoint what we're doing wrong to unknowingly sabotage our financial future. For example, the copy reads:

- The Eight Biggest Mistakes Investors Make … and How to Avoid Them
- How a simple diversification mistake can cost you a fortune
- The most serious retirement-planning error you can make
- Why investing only in U.S. companies can dramatically reduce returns
- Why NOT losing money is as important as making it
- Why you may be using investment strategies that are actually working against you

Don't these pique your curiosity? Hmmm, what mistakes could I be making? At what cost? How can I prevent them? And this report is going to tell me all that for FREE? Why wouldn't I call this toll-free number and order this booklet?

Please note: I am not addressing the validity of the information in this booklet (I've never ordered it.) And I am NOT suggesting we "go over to the dark side" and write manipulative sales copy that hammers away at the fear emotions.

I am suggesting that most descriptions I see of articles, books, and online reports tend to emphasize only the soft "How to's" that don't carry the same urgency and incentive. How to … fulfill your dream, be a better supervisor, improve your health, clean your desk, lead a better quality life. Yes, those are appealing ... but are you motivated to get out your wallet and order a special report on those topics, right now?

Your description will compel more people to sit up, pay attention and purchase your learning resources if you ask yourself, "What are they afraid of? What could they be doing that's undermining their success? What mistakes could be costing them their job, marriage, or health?" Include some of those bullet points in your sales copy and people will be more motivated to ACT NOW, instead of someday when they get around to it.

2. **Create a Measurable Methodology to make your Ideas Proprietary.**

This is an important point because if you incorporate your best-practice tips into regular paragraphs, they will blend in with all your other information and get lost in the text. Brilliant ideas can get missed if they're not spotlighted, named and numbered.

Would Stephen Covey's book *The 7 Habits of Highly Effective People* have broken out and endured if he hadn't numbered those habits? Imagine if he had just shared his observations about how people could be more effective in several hundred pages. How could we remember his conclusions? How could we apply them?

One of the reasons Stephen Covey has made a lot of money licensing people in his methodology is because he made his information proprietary. He identified a specific number of steps and gave them interesting sound-bite names "Start with the end in mind," "Seek first to understand," "Sharpen the saw." We can learn from his example.

Notice I have numbered the steps in this book – 26 Ways to Monetize Your Mind. Imagine if you had just read a 130+ page book with no separate chapters, no numbered tips, no Table of Contents with an identifiable structure. These ideas would have gotten all jumbled together.

IDEApreneur

Giving your information a framework makes it digestible and distinctive. Even if there are hundreds of books or articles on the same topic, none will be similar to yours. You have taken your material to a higher level by crafting it into a visual format that belongs to you. Numbering and naming your idea's steps, principles or keys makes your content easier to grasp, remember and own.

This is even more important on e-products. If product buyers just print out page after page of information with no discernible structure, it's hard to keep all that information straight in your head. Breaking your copy into "read-bites" with bullet points and numbered steps will make your material seem more substantive, factual, and "meaty."

You can turn your idea into a step-by-step methodology by asking yourself:

- What are 5 things I know for sure about this topic?
- What are 3 aspects of this subject that are non-negotiable?
- What 7 steps do people need to take in this process?
- What are 4 pragmatic ways to correct this problem?
- What are 10 do's and don'ts I can suggest regarding this idea?
- What 6 actions can people take to stop doing this wrong and start doing it better?

Do you see how, by pre-supposing a certain number of tips you'll give customers, audience members, readers or purchases, you can generate a point-by-point system that belongs to you and you alone? Now, your advice is specific and can be replicated. Numbering your ideas gives them immediate added value because they don't seem generic.

You can also self-publish your:

- blogs through Wordpress – https://wordpress.com/create
- e-books via Create Space on Amazon – https://www.createspace.com

- e-books on SmashWords – https://www.smashwords.com/about/how_to_publish_on_smashwords who will get your e-book up on Barnes and Noble and multiple digital platforms.

I've known Mark Coker, the founder of SmashWords, for a decade (we were both friends of self-publishing legend Dan Poynter) and can vouch for his integrity and his commitment to providing helpful services to first-time authors.

Bud Garner, co-author of *Chicken Soup for the Author's Soul*, was a popular speaker at Maui Writers Conference, which I emceed for 17 years. Bud was fond of saying, "When you speak, your words echo across the room. But when you write, your words echo across the ages."

If you want your idea to leave a legacy, write about it via blogs, articles and books. It is a guarantee your idea will get out in the world, positively impact people you'll never meet, and scale its enduring influence. And if you're thinking, "I'm not a writer." You don't have to have an English or Creative Writing degree to write quality blogs, special reports or books. If you're an IDEApreneur, you're passionate about your idea and you have expertise or knowledge that could inspire, educate or enlighten others. Ask a colleague to interview you about your idea and turn that into an e-book.

Or, take a voice recorder with you when you walk and TALK OUT your book. Story-board the points, examples and suggestions you want to make and then talk out the book, a chapter at a time. I've had several clients who were "busy" and who didn't have time to sit down and write talk out their books, 15 minutes here on a plane, 15 minutes there during a workout.

They had their voice recordings transcribed and then they turned over the draft to a professional editor or book doctor or cleaned it up themselves. The beauty of this approach is it expedites the writing process and ensures your writing has your voice, passion and knowledge intact.

Questions to Ask – Actions to Take

1. Do you like to write? Would you consider yourself a good writer? What writing have you already done on your idea? How has it helped to spread the word about it already?
2. Could you outline two articles you'd like to write – or story-board the chapters you'd like to include in a book about your idea – and start "talking them out" when you're walking/talking?
3. When will you research Wordpress, SmashWords or Create Space to explore selfpublishing blogs and e-books so you can get your ideas out of your head and into the world – where they can make a positive difference for others – and a prosperous living for you?

CHAPTER 23
Get Interviewed by Media on Your Idea

"Let's give 'em something to talk about"
– Lyrics by **Bonnie Raitt**

I KNOW there must be some publicists out there who do a good job for their clients.

Unfortunately, I have heard from hundreds of IDEApreneurs, authors, speakers and business owners over the years who have spent five figures on publicists with minimal results.

It's not necessarily the publicists' fault. You can send press releases to TV, radio, print and online media all day long – it just doesn't necessarily mean they're going to book you for their talk show, interview you on their program or podcast, print your article or review your book.

I'll always remember one completely discouraged colleague, a well-respected consultant with Fortune 500 clients, who had written a business book on ethics.

He believed his book had the potential to break out since the Enron scandal was in the news every day, so he decided to invest $50,000 (yes, that's four zeroes) for three months of book publicity with a well-known New York public relations firm.

Three months later. Nothing. Not one TV appearance. Not one radio interview. Not one book review. He flew to New York to talk with the head of the company. "How can this be?" he asked. "How can a quality book from a major publisher on a hot topic not receive any media coverage?"

Do you know what the owner of the PR agency said? "These things take time. Sign up for another three months and we'll figure out what's wrong and fix it."

Yikes.

Now, if you're a large company or a well-funded entrepreneur with millions of dollars of revenue or venture capital; by all means hire a PR specialist, marketing team, or advertising agency with a proven track record to get you in the news and keep you there.

Or, if you know a trusted publicist who has measurable results and has produced impressive coverage for a colleague; go ahead and explore if they work on a pay-for-results basis.

If you're on a budget, I suggest YOU become your own publicist. Here's how.

1. Read a major metropolitan daily such as the *Washington Post, Chicago Tribune, Los Angeles Times,* and business newspapers such as your local Business Journal or *Investors Business Daily*.

Also read the online publications that are relevant to your idea and area of expertise such as *Huffington Post, BlogHer, Forbes, Fast Company, Entrepreneur, Success* and *INC*.

I have been partial to *USA TODAY* because it had its finger on the pulse of POP! culture and was delivered free to many hotels around the country so you reached a target audience of business travelers who are often decision-makers who have the power and money to hire you as a consultant, or contract you to bring your ideas to their association or company.

2. Look for headlines related to your idea. For example, if your idea is a new way to deal with bullies, there could be a pictograph about a

new study reporting alarming statistics about increasing violence in schools. There could be an article about bully bosses in the Money section or how to deal with out-of-control relatives at holiday dinners in an advice column in Style.

3. Email the reporter (their email address or contact information is often at the end of the article or in the newspaper info box on the inside 2nd page) and compliment them on a specific point they made. This is crucial to this process. You don't just want to pitch your idea. You want first to cite a specific comment in the article that was insightful, provocative, or welcomed.

4. Pose a "Did you know?" question. Expand upon a point the reporter made by asking if s/he knows about another survey just released that indicates even more startling evidence of this problem. Elaborate upon a quote in the article by asking if s/he would like to be connected with other sources/experts on that topic. Ask if s/he is aware of a related trend in another industry?

Why is this important? You already have an interested party – a qualified prospect - because this reporter has spent time on this topic. Instead of making the equivalent of a "cold call," you're gifting someone who has already demonstrated they care about this subject with a newsworthy insight that would warrant a follow-up article or a more updated, in-depth treatment of the idea.

5. Say, "You may be wondering about my credentials." Whatever you do, don't mention your book, product, cause or idea first.

Why? They'll immediately conclude you just want to shill your book or sell your idea/produce/cause and will shut down. And don't make sweeping subjective claims such as, "I'm an internationally respected consultant with clients all over the world." Says who?

Instead, offer 3 brief pragmatic examples of your expertise with names and numbers that prove your platform. For example, "My bully prevention program is used in more than 20 school districts including Fairfax County; I've interviewed more than 100 teachers and principals, and my book has been endorsed by the National Education Association."

By the way, if you are an active blogger and have a large social media following, BE SURE TO MENTION IT. Media understands the importance of a large "digital platform" and welcome a chance to get their magazine, newspaper, TV/radio show, podcast in front of even more people.

6. Offer, "I would be glad to share some tips, stories, recent research findings and recommendations on this topic that would be of interest and value to your readers."

Please notice that nowhere in this conversation have you said, "I'd like to send you my book." Or, "I want to be on your show." **The focus is not on you.** The focus is on helping this journalist produce an article, TV/radio show, podcast or blog that will be beneficial to their readers and viewers.

7. You might want to mention, "You can trust me to speak in sound-bites, and to have a same day response." This is rare and welcome. Reporters often need short turn-around times as they work on tight deadlines so they like to have a list of go-to-experts they can count on to be ready on short notice. They will come back to you again and again as long as they can count on you for a pithy sound-bite that will add value and make "good copy."

8. Gauge their interest. If they're ready to get off the call (or if you're leaving a voice message and it's important to keep this under 90 seconds long), simply say, "Thank you for your time and for keeping me in mind as a resource on this topic. If you'd like, I'll be glad to send you some provocative quotes or story ideas about this topic you are welcome to keep on file for future articles and shows."

9. If you end up having a conversation and they seem interested, then you can add, "Would you like an autographed copy of my book?" or "Would you like a list of "7 Things to NEVER Say to a Bully" that you are welcome to feature in a future podcast or show?" Don't give them the impression you're going to spam them with material or drown them in press releases. Offer to send ONE item that will be of use to them if they ever want to re-visit this topic.

A single mom in my book camp who was on a tight budget said, "Does this same system work with TV and radio stations and popular podcasters and big-name bloggers?"

I told her, "Yes, with a few modifications. I've had clients and colleagues who have pitched national shows such as *Oprah, Today Show, Good Morning America, Forbes, INC, 60 Minutes, 20/20*. John Lee Dumas and *Entrepreneur on Fire* were interviewed as a result."

I cautioned her, "Please understand getting on a national show if you're not a celebrity is the exception, not the rule. To get on one of these top-ranked shows, you usually need a national name, luck, an idea whose 'time has come' and/or good timing. I believe in the 'You-Never-Know-Factor" and it's true that media miracles do indeed happen.

"For example, I have a colleague, Leslie Charles, who sent a press release about her book *Why is Everyone So Cranky?* to Nightline which happened to be received by a producer who had a really cantankerous boss so she was motivated to do a segment on that topic and flew Leslie to NYC for an interview. So, serendipity (or as I like to call it, Seren-Destiny) does happen.

"However, for most people who are not famous, it can be a daunting task to try to get national media attention. If you have limited time and funds, the process of sending unsolicited pitches, press releases and media packets to national shows doesn't always pay off commensurately in results.

As IDEApreneurs, we need to triage our time to make sure we focus on High-ROI (Return on Investment) priorities. That's why, instead of sending out mass press releases to national shows (which often don't get read), I recommend you **approach your local network affiliates**.

And, instead of sending "blind" pitches asking to be on their show or announcing the publication of your book or the launch of your business or cause, increase the likelihood of a favorable response by focusing on how you can serve their audience.

You can do this by a) capitalizing on a CURRENT topic they've recently covered and by b) positioning yourself as a topic expert they can use in the future as a trusted go-to resource. It is so rare for producers to receive prepared offers of assistance that genuinely focus on providing value to their viewers and listeners, they are often motivated to say yes.

Here are the specific steps to doing this.

1. Watch local network affiliate (ABC, NBC, CBS, FOX) TV programs your target audience watches. This could be morning or evening news shows or local entertainment shows (such as *Good Morning Seattle*).

2. When you see a program or segment on "your" subject, call the station that day or the next day and ask to be connected to the producer of the show. Don't ask to speak with the talk show host or the broadcast anchor because they often don't make the decisions about which guests appear on their show. The producers are usually the ones who select the topics, line up the experts, etc.

3. Whether you get voice mail or a "live person," start off with "I know you're busy and may I have one minute of your time?" Producers are usually very busy. If you just start talking, they will probably cut you off because they have no idea if you're going to try to talk their ear off. If you ask for one minute, they'll probably gruffly agree, "One minute" which is why you prepare your pitch in advance so you can get to the

point concisely and compellingly.

4. Repeat steps 4-7 from the steps covered earlier in this chapter on how to earn the favorable interest and trust of journalists.

5. Most TV segments are 3-7 minutes long, max. Guests often get cut off mid-sentence because the host has to cut to a commercial. If that happened to a previous guest who was being interviewed on your idea or topic, you might want to say, "Toward the end of the interview with ___ yesterday, the host asked this question and your guest didn't have time to respond fully. I'd be glad to do a follow-up show where we go into detail about that specific issue." Or, if this is a print interview, you can refer to a recent article and mention an important point that was given short shrift, "Kudos on your column on Monday about ___. You had mentioned this __, and I was wondering if you knew about the report that came out from NIH last week?"

6. If you can be available on short notice, be sure to mention that. Many local TV shows want local topic experts they can count on to show up with only a few hours' notice and give an informed sound-bite on late breaking news.

The good news is, with this approach, you can generate national press coverage without spending a lot of money. I know this from experience as two clients, Carl and Deb Potter from Oklahoma City, have done just that.

The Potters are internationally known safety consultants for electric utilities (talk about a cornering a niche!) They wanted to expand their speaking/consulting to other industries so they used the approach described in this chapter. They kept their eyes peeled for headlines about safety in national newspapers – and found it when NASA revealed that some astronauts had been discovered having some drinks before a space mission.

The Potters immediately contacted reporters to point out that workers in many blue-collar professions have a tradition of "going out for a cold one after work" which can jeopardize their safety the next day.

They also pointed out that many avid football fans show up on Monday with a hangover after putting away a six-pack of beer at the Sunday football game. The Potters then offered examples of how drinking the night before work can negatively impact productivity and can actually put coworkers and customers at risk.

As a result, the Potters received national media attention which has further established them as topic experts, generated speaking engagements from new associations and justified a raise in their consulting fees.

And if your efforts pay off and you get booked for an interview, be sure to study the techniques earlier in this book about how to share repeatable, retweetable sound-bites so your insights get quoted and take your idea viral.

Questions to Ask – Actions to Take

1. Have you ever been interviewed on TV, radio or for a newspaper or magazine before? If so, how did it go? Did it help get your cause, idea, business, product some well-deserved attention?
2. How are you going to follow up on these steps to get your idea in the news? Are you going to read publications that appeal to your ideal customers and reach out to journalists who have written about your topic? Are you going to contact producers at your local affiliates? Explain.
3. Have you prepared some relevant, repeatable, retweetable sound-bites to increase the likelihood that your idea's message will go viral and you'll be asked back? What are they?

CHAPTER 24
Scale Your Idea's Visibility Via Strategic Social Media

"Smart phones and social media expand our universe. We can connect with others and collect information easier and faster than ever."
– Daniel Goleman

TO PARAPHRASE author/psychologist Daniel Goleman:

Social media expands our IDEA'S universe. We can connect with our ideal customers and share our IDEA'S information easier and faster than ever.

That said. We need to be smart about social media.

As psychologist Neil Strauss said, **"Because it's so easy to medicate our need for selfworth by pandering to win followers, 'likes' and view counts, social media has become the métier of choice for many people who might otherwise channel that energy into books, music, art, – or even their own Web ventures."**

Ouch.

That's why I'm going to share my best practices about how we can triage and leverage our time on social media so everything we do is a strategic ROI.

Sam Horn

The goal is not to fall prey to the addiction of checking our stats every other ten minutes.

The goal is to use this miraculous platform to get our idea's message out to even more people – in ways that add value for all involved.

If it seems like just about everyone is using social media these days, you'd be right.

For example, our President's *dog* has two twitter accounts (@WhiteHousePooch and @BoObamasDog) with 23,000+ followers.

Fortunately, there are ways to gain favorable attention and traction for yourself and your ideas, even in such a crowded marketplace. Please note; these are *not* your basic tips on how to set up social media accounts nor is this a comprehensive manual with everything you need to know.

If you're looking for a guide on how to get started with social media, you might want to check (http://mashable.com/guidebook/twitter/) which frequently updates their instructions to stay on top of the latest trends, developments and innovations.

With that being said, let's get social:

1. **Maintain a Triple S Social Media Balance.**

We all know someone we've "unliked" because all they ever did was spam us with their unwanted opinions, me-me-me adventures, or high-pressure sales offers. Don't be that guy.

It's in your best interests to keep a SERVE – SHOWCASE – SELL balance.

SERVE – Offer interesting, inspiring, enlightening useful information relevant to your idea.

SHOWCASE – Feature OTHER PEOPLE'S useful, inspiring insights relevant to your idea.

SELL – Announce offerings of programs, products, services, projects related to your idea.

Be sure to NEVER send out several SELL posts in a row. That's off-putting and people will quickly decide to block you. And yes, I'm suggesting you showcase the work of respected colleagues. You want to be seen as a resource for wisdom on your area of expertise – and that includes featuring recent research, quality books, compelling insights from others in your field.

You can be a curator and collector of current information, recent research and best-practices about your idea. That does not detract from people's respect for you – it increases their respect because you're being an advocate and ambassador for the value of your idea, topic, cause.

People will look forward to your Tweets, Facebook posts, LinkedIn blogs, etc. because they never know what they're going to find – but they know it's going to be a good use of their time.

2. **Metrics Matter.**

Tracking social media via TweetDeck or Hootsuite is *the* secret to leveraging your time spent on social media and staying on top of when you and your idea are in the news or buzzfeed. Why?

I co-hosted an event at USA TODAY headquarters with Jennifer Abernethy, author of *The Complete Idiot's Guide to Social Media Marketing* (a great resource that will teach you every single detail of how to make the most of your time online).

Jennifer said in passing, "Hey Sam, that's great news about Todd of CEO READ loving your book POP!" I looked at her in amazement, "WHAT?!" I had no idea what she was talking about. She said, "He tweeted it."

I never knew. Because I wasn't on Tweetdeck. I wasn't tracking my book title, my name, my key words on Tweetdeck so I never saw that Tweet until Jennifer brought it to my attention.

Missed opportunity because this had happened several months before. If I had immediately Tweeted back a thank-you, who knows what that might have led to? An interview or feature on the homepage of their website? A Change This Manifesto that went out to their millions of subscribers - business decision-makers around the country - who buy books in bulk for their employees? A presentation at their annual conference or a recommendation to other events?

You'll never know what's reaching and resonating with your target audience unless you do analytics analysis of some kind – whether that's through Google Analytics (free!), Hootsuite or Salesforce to track your Facebook and Twitter results. These easy-to-use tools make it easy to track what people are looking at, for how long, and what they're choosing to share with others.

3. **Plan your posts with your ideal customers in mind.**

For example, what's the best time to post social media for you? If your target audience is stay-at-home moms, your target time might be anywhere from 8:30 AM to 11:30 AM during a weekday. Why? Because it's right after they've dropped off the kids at school and have some "me" time before starting the work for the day. If you post at the optimal time for a white collar worker (4-5 PM on Friday right before the weekend), you would completely miss your "mom" demographic because that's when the kids are getting home and she's too busy to pay attention to social media.

4. **Be real. Be you**.

No one wants to follow a robot. And no one want to feel you're using social media simply to further your agenda. Social media is about having conversations with your target audience.

Look up the celebrities and personalities with the most followers, e.g., Ashton Kutcher. Guy Kawasaki. Dan Pink. Brene Brown. They're the ones who respond to, and interact with, their fans. You want to be approachable and occasionally share personal information that's relevant. If you're only tweeting out business articles and how-to blogs, or only re-tweeting other people, you don't seem like you care about the person following you other than the fact that it increased your follower count (or worse yet, you're just lazy).

With their permission, I occasionally include posts of my travels with my friends and updates about my sister, sons and their wives and yes, even my very cute grandson. Those are almost always my most "liked" posts because it's what people yearn for these days – genuine connection with people on and off the job, the whole person – instead of just business-related posts that have commercial intentions only.

5. **Follow people you respect and who you want to be associated with.**

Quick. Who are the ten people in the world you most respect? They could be visionaries, journalists, thought-leaders, inventors, musicians, artists, authors, athletes, entrepreneurs, politicians, preachers, musicians, icons in your industry. Are you following them? If so, good for you. If not, go online right now and follow them.

Why is this important? We want to enlarge our perception of what social media is. It's like having a library at our finger-tips. The world's greatest people are a click away.

To be an IDEApreneur, you see the world as material. Your life is your lab. The more people you study who are powerful, proactive and positive – the more it seeps into your own work.

Use social media to expose yourself to the best of humankind. Be inspired by their wisdom, by what they're saying and doing that is ADVANCING all that's good in the world. Share their work. In taking responsibility for spreading the word about good work, you are integrating it into who you are, how you show up, how you're perceived – all of which is a win for your idea.

Don't automatically follow everyone back who follows you. Be discerning. Look at this person's lists to see if you share interests, values, contacts and if they are the quality of person you want to be associated with.

6. Make 'em look with visuals.

Words alone – even well-thought-out, quality words – may not be enough to earn someone's attention. Always include a photo with your Tweets and Facebook posts. It triples its odds of catching people's eye and motivating them to read your post and/or click on the link.

Be very careful to use only copyright-free images. If you use ShutterStock or Getty images in your posts and don't have a paid account with them, their attorney could get in touch (years later!) to collect royalties for using their images without permission or payment.

The best way to get around the copyright laws is to use your own images. The cameras on smart phones have such high quality resolution, you can use them in most posts and they're YOURS.

Check out how photographer Dewitt Jones uses his brilliant images on social media to maintain a thriving and profitable business from … Molokai.

You can use a free "editor" site like www.canva.com to create a picture quote that embeds your idea into an image that's the best of all worlds. Ensure that your logo, website or twitter handle is on the image so that curious clickers can find you to find out more.

This may seem obvious, but make sure your image matches your content. A beautiful waterfall might draw attention, but not if the quote embedded in it doesn't match and if it's not relevant to your business audience. Steer clear of clip art and generic images that dehumanize your connection. Real-live, "believable" human beings motivate people to put themselves "in your story" and to relate to you and your idea.

7. **Schedule posts so you don't have to be a "slave" of social media.**

I can't tell you how many people tell me they "hate" social media – or they don't want to be a "slave" to it. IDEApreneurs don't want to be – and can't afford to be - on Twitter or Facebook all the time. You have work to do!

That's why it's smart to use programs like Hootsuite to schedule tweets for specific times of the day. Blog posts, videos and images are all great examples of posts that can be pre-scheduled. Never use an auto-reply program. If you get a mass influx of followers it becomes really obvious that you're not the one taking the time to send a personal message to each follower.

Plus, here's one place it's wise to get ahead of yourself. Save up content for rainy days.

Maybe you're on vacation, meeting a tight deadline, or having a day of fun with your family and friends. Keep an archives of always-relevant (not date specific) content that can be sent out so your idea stays visible and you stay connected – even when you're not around.

8. Don't operate in social media silos. Multi-purpose content to maximize its value.

Some clients tell me, "Blogging is a waste of time. No one ever comments on them." I tell them, "Blogging can be a waste of time if you're simply writing to a captive audience who is already familiar with your work. It is an investment of time if you're connecting with new people who are unfamiliar with your work."

The way to do that is to pull three sound-bites out of every blog and turn them into questions that you send out on different days via Facebook and Twitter. For example, I wrote a blog about "See Speaking as a Sport." But I didn't stop there. I then tweeted, "What if we saw speaking as a sport?" included a photo, a link to the blog and a hashtag of @Toastmasters. Boom. That one tweet went out to the hundreds of thousands of followers of #Toastmasters.

Later that day, I excerpted the first paragraph of the post that talked about how a successful entrepreneur was having panic attacks while preparing for an important presentation, asked people if they still found themselves nervous when speaking, and would they like to know how to walk into any speech or pitch with confidence, Facebooked it with a new photo and a link.

In a couple days, I sent another tweet asking, "Are you a 'gimmee' the ball kind of person?" and included a new photo of a basketball player holding a ball with a link to the article which is on how we can step up with a, "Gimmee the ball" attitude when the speaking game's on the line.

One blog – leveraged three different ways via Facebook and Twitter – for a minimum amount of time and thousands of clicks, reads and visits to my blog/website. Is that worth it? You bet it is.

Questions to Ask – Actions to Take

1. Are you already active on social media? Which accounts? Facebook? Twitter? Pinterest? LinkedIn? YouTube? How much time do you spend on social media daily?
2. What *tangible* rewards has being on social media brought you and your idea? How has it produced sales? Connected you with customers? Generated business opportunities?
3. What are three of these ideas you're going to use to scale the visibility and traction of your idea and business? What policies and practices are you going to put in place to make sure your time spent on social media is an ROI for you – and for your fans and followers?

SECTION VI
Ensure Ongoing Success

"If you really want to do it, you'll find a way. If you don't, you'll find an excuse." - **Jim Rohn**

THIS BOOK has given you 24 ways to monetize your mind and turn ideas into income.

I'm about to share two of the most important ways to follow up on your good intentions and make your idea a profitable reality.

Please don't try to do all this yourself. Turning an ephemeral idea into a tangible reality takes time, energy, determination, perseverance and a variety of helping hands and heads.

The next chapter shows how to create your own accountability group to create much-needed support and synergy that can expedite your

IDEApreneur process and make it more enjoyable. And our final chapter digs deep into why all your efforts will be worthwhile.

You can tell by now that I love quotes. They really are a way of capturing enduring wisdom in a few pithy, profound words.

Of all the quotes I know, this is my favorite, and it has been my favorite for 30+ years.

"The purpose of life isn't to be happy; it's to matter; to feel that it's made some difference that you have lived at all." - Leo Rosten

I don't think Mr. Rosten is saying it's not important to be happy. It IS important to be happy. It's just not the *purpose* of life.

The purpose of life is, as Rosten says, to feel that we are serving, contributing, adding value … that in some way, there is someone who is a little better off because we've been here.

Ideas turned into tangible products, programs, businesses and books can accomplish that.

Chapter 26 can help you tap into your "why" (as Simon Sinek would say), so you are grounded in a *purpose* for being an IDEApreneur that carries you forward to success – no matter what you encounter along the way. I hope you find it inspiring.

CHAPTER 25
Set-up an IDEA Accountability Group for Support, Synergy and Results

"You think you're lost but you're not lost on your own. You're not alone. I will stand by you, I will help you through when you've done all you can do."
– Rascal Flatts

I HAD THE PRIVILEGE of hosting the non-fiction retreat at the Maui Writers Conference for years.

What a joy it was, there on the shore of the Pacific Ocean in beautiful Wailea, doing a deep dive into everyone's project, brainstorming and strategizing how to create a quality book that would encourage, inspire, educate and enlighten.

No one wanted to leave, so we scheduled a group call a month after the retreat to re-connect with updates. As each of our 18 participants shared their progress, a common theme emerged.

One woman summed it up eloquently. "I miss our community. It was such a luxury spending that week with kindred spirits who shared similar goals. It was easy to stay focused because we spent all day, every day, talking about our manuscripts, swapping best-practices, and learning how to be better writers and get our message out into the world. It was bliss.

"Now that I'm back home, I'm pulled in ten different directions. Some days I sit down to write and I've got a hundred other thoughts and responsibilities swirling in my head. Other times I just sit there and stare at the screen and nothing comes. Other days I produce pages but then look at them and don't know if they're any good. Help?"

Patricia had just articulated every **IDEApreneur's conundrum.** As film director George Lucas said, "I wish there were ten of me and we could each be doing what we wanted to do."

How do we persevere on our IDEApreneurial project when we have so many obligations tugging at us? How do we stay motivated over the long haul of ups and downs that accompany any creative endeavor? How can we supply the discipline to finish what we start?

Working in isolation means we have to supply our own "wind beneath our mental wings." Unless we're fortunate to have a supportive significant other, no one is giving us the encouragement that what we're doing matters, that it serves a greater purpose and it's worth persevering. Going solo means there's no one to cheer us up when we're down, no one to congratulate us when we receive good news, no one to hold us accountable and give us a swift kick in the okole (Hawaiian for rump) when we're procrastinating.

I spoke at a small business conference years ago and remember a representative from the SBA telling the group **the #1 challenge entrepreneurs face is *not* running out of money, it's running out of energy and commitment.**

Studies show a surprising number of small business owners find that working for themselves is not as fun, glamorous or satisfying as they anticipated. They go back to working for an organization because they miss the structure, support and socialization that accompanies working alongside other people.

Furthermore, a challenge every IDEApreneur faces is we get so close to our work, we can't see it clearly anymore. You've heard the saying, "You can't see the forest for the trees?" Well, we can't see the project for the pages. We get so immersed; we lose our objectivity. We have no idea if our work's good or destined for the trash. It can be hard working in a vacuum of feedback and support.

So, what to do? Form an idea accountability group.

Quite frankly, this is single best thing I've done to advance my career in the last 10 years. It has contributed to a personal satisfaction and a professional success I never could have achieved on my own. Furthermore, it has been a source of great fun, joy, and insight. My master-mind buddies are a blessing I am grateful for on a daily basis.

I'll briefly share how I discovered the power of master-mind groups, and then share tips on how you can set up an idea accountability group that's a win for everyone involved. Please note: these aren't hard-and-fast rules – they're simply guidelines to save you trial-and-terror learning so you don't have to re-invent the wheel in creating your own group.

I had the privilege of living in Hawaii for 17 years. As much as I loved living in Paradise, I didn't realize how professionally isolating it was until I moved to the Mainland and had the good fortune to share a room with Rebecca Morgan, (co-founder of SpeakerNetNews.com – the first anthology online newsletter serving the professional speaking community - reaching 10,000 people worldwide), at the National Speakers Association convention.

We had so much fun sharing/swapping notes from the different sessions and brainstorming how we could grow our careers, we decided to continue this rewarding collaboration following the conference. We invited five carefully selected peers to join us in monthly phone calls and twice a-year in-person meetings.

At our first meeting, we were "going around the table" updating each other on our priority projects and pinpointing where and how we could use help.

When it was my turn, I told everyone, "I'm thoroughly enjoying this and I'm glad to be part of it, but I can't think of anything I need help with so I'll just donate my time back to the group."

There was silence for a moment and then Mariah Burton Nelson (bless her heart) said, "Well, what projects are you working on right now?"

"I'm re-doing my website," I told them.

"We can help you with that," Mariah said confidently.

And she was right. A half hour later, my website was infinitely better because of the group's insightful suggestions. **My subsequent epiphany was, "It had been so long since I had asked for help, I had forgotten how."**

Since there hadn't been any other professional speakers on Maui when I lived there, I didn't have anyone to "talk shop" with. The few times I did share my business goals and activities with other people, they simply didn't have the industry knowledge to be able to give informed advice. So, I stopped asking. I ended up operating independently and doing everything myself. And that worked pretty well. As the saying goes, it was what it was.

But after that first experience with the Master Mind group (and every meeting since), I realized that **six heads are definitely better than one**.

For example, I was discussing an online info-product I was developing and Rebecca asked, "Why are you only offering one option? Why not bundle your CD's together and offer three different packages so people can buy at their own comfort level?"

Uh, duh. Why wasn't I doing that? Never occurred to me. That's just one of the many perks gained from other people bringing their objective perspective. They can often pinpoint exactly what needs to be done to take your project to the next level.

So, ready to find out how to set up your own idea accountability group? I have collected our best practice tips – and interviewed other virtual action groups to ask what works and what doesn't. I've distilled that information into the following 18 suggestions. I hope they help you gather a group of like-minded people to support you in fast-forwarding your creative projects.

1. Seek a group of individuals who have a similar skill and/or experience level. The group doesn't have to be geographically local. It's more important to invite bright people who have common interests and goals, yet bring different talents to the table. For example, someone might be good with finance, another with e-commerce, another with marketing, etc. The primary purpose is for everyone to be committed to being supportive and action-oriented.

Please note: The reason you don't want wildly different skill levels is this is not intended to be a mentoring group. If your more experienced members always end up teaching the rest of the group, that results in an unfair balance in the give-take that eventually dooms the group. You want everyone to be able to contribute, receive and benefit equally so the group is quid pro quo.

The best group size is usually 5 to 6 members. If the intent is to focus on work-related projects, feel free to have a mix of men and women. If the group is designed to focus on both personal and professional matters, you might elect to have the same gender so everyone's comfortable discussing intimate issues.

2. Clarify a common goal and/or primary purpose and select group members accordingly. For example, some IDEApreneur groups focus on the start-up stage where the individuals are trying to get funding and get their projects off the ground. Other groups are for experienced IDEApreneurs who already have a business and who want to grow revenue and scale the size of their organization or launch other products. Some groups don't care what type of idea you're working on; their goal is simply to help each other finish it by a certain deadline. These groups often welcome a cross-pollination of different talents, styles

and genres because it adds value by offering a variety of perspectives. Other groups prefer that everyone is working in the same field or space – like healthcare, bio-med, retail, financial services, online products – so they can go deep into that industry's specific needs.

Agree to the frequency of meetings. Most groups meet by phone for 90 minutes every six weeks and in-person twice a year. Once a month comes around pretty fast – and every two months is too far apart. Every six weeks is just about right.

3. Use a bridge line, Skype, GoToMeeting or Google hangouts for your phone meetings. These resources are FREE – or available for a minimal fee – and you can be looking at documents while you're talking to your fellow masterminders.

4. Rotate the facilitator each time to keep the division of duties equitable. The facilitator's job is to remind people of the date and time of the call, and request confirmations RSVP's. Then, email the agenda to everyone reflecting the divvied-up time and a reminder of the call-in number and code three days before the call.

During the meeting, the facilitator's role is to start and end on time, welcome everyone and firmly and fairly enforce the agenda and move the conversations forward so everyone gets their "full" time to discuss their priority and receive feedback.

5. Start each meeting with a short 2 minute personal "report in." This is an opportunity to share non-business updates and highlights so the group connects with each other on a holistic level. This builds a sense of community and provides an upbeat way to begin each call.

6. Divvy up the available remaining time so each individual has an equal amount of time to brainstorm a priority of their choice. You have autonomy during "your time" to share a challenge, ask for feedback, bounce ideas off the group to get their perspective about how to pro-

ceed on a HIGH ROI project – whatever will deliver the most value for you.

7. Limit the number of pages each member can mail to the group for review prior to each meeting. It's important to have policies about this. In a prior group, one individual violated this rule by sending the group three different slide decks and asking which one they preferred. Yikes. A standard policy is each member can email up to 3 pages of material to other members and this needs to be received at least 3 days in advance of the call so everyone can study it before the call.

8. When it's "your turn," **always ask for specific feedback. Say, "What would really be helpful for me is if you . . ." and then tell exactly what clarity you're seeking regarding your priority.** The more precise you are about what you want/need, the more likely you are to get incisive input that will take your project to the next level. If you're vague when requesting advice, the group won't know what you're looking for and their responses will be all over the map.

9. Agree to give constructive vs. critical feedback. My mom used to say, "Encouragement is oxygen for the soul." Sometimes we are feeling fragile about our work and we would be devastated by negative feedback. If that's how you feel, say so. Instead of simply pointing out what is wrong with someone's project or what you *don't like*, focus first on what you liked, what is working well, and then suggest how this idea could be even more effective or profitable.

10. An important ground-rule is, "When it's someone's time, stay focused on *their* project." This may sound obvious; it's not. The facilitator needs to enforce this rule so one domineering member doesn't hi-jack the discussion and keep bringing it back to him or herself. That means not starting sentences with, "*I'm* going through the same thing, I can't seem to figure out …" An easy way to stay focused on other people's priorities is to use the word "you" more than "I."

11. A non-negotiable ground-rule is that everyone agrees to keep discussions confidential. This means no sharing details with family or close friends. This is essential for group members to feel safe revealing private concerns. Adopt the Las Vegas motto: "What's discussed here stays here."

12. **An important requirement is that everyone commits to showing up every time**. My research found the primary reason master-mind groups fall apart is members start missing meetings. There will always be legitimate reasons we "just can't make it this time." Unfortunately, as soon as no-shows start happening, a dangerous precedent is set that eventually undermines the carefully woven fabric of the community. It sets up an inequity that gradually destroys the unity of the group. Everyone needs to agree this is an investment they're making in themselves, their ideas and their careers which means they show up – even when it's expensive, inconvenient or tempting to back out due to a busy schedule or other priorities.

13. Individuals must feel comfortable giving candid feedback, when asked for it. Yes, the emphasis is on being constructive; however, that doesn't mean holding back honest observations if it seems a member is going down a destructive path. As one of my master-mind buddies once said, "I trust my accountability group to tell me what I need to hear – even if I may not want to hear it at the time. I mean, if I can't count on them to give it to me straight, how else will I know I'm doing something counter-productive?"

14. You may want to preface "tough love" feedback with, "May I have permission to give some unwelcome news?" or "I have some reservations about whether this is the best course of action. Do you want to hear them?" or "Have you researched this vendor's track record? I know several former clients who felt they were over-charged and the company didn't deliver on its promises."

15. **Schedule a pipeline of meetings up to six months in advance.** This "locks in" your dates so you can save them on your calendar and prevent double-bookings. I interviewed dozens of groups about which day and time seems to have the fewest conflicts. The "winner" seems to be Sunday evening - 8:00 pm (EST) - 5:00 pm (PST)

16. Establish guidelines for "off-line" email communication. You may want to agree to assign priority numbers to your emails in the subject heading so group members can quickly assess their importance. For example:

#1 = Urgent email. Please look at this today. I really need your input.

#2 = Please look at this before our next call/meeting

#3 = FYI for your interest - if you have time and want to look at it.

Most groups forbid CC'ing jokes and mass-mailed, spam-like chain letters no matter how "cute." And many groups agree not to send messages of a political, religious or fund-raising nature.

17. Clarify the group's policy about off-line "consulting" so no one takes advantage of a member's normally paid-for expertise. It's smart to establish a rule governing how often members can request each other's professional advice (accountant, intellectual property attorney, doctor, marketing expert, tech/website/social media talents) outside of scheduled get-togethers.

Our group developed a rule in which we can request one 15 minute "consulting" call every three months to access each other's specialized expertise. When 15 minutes is up, the discussion is over unless we'd like to pay their normal hourly rate. This may sound unnecessarily strict; however, it places parameters on picking our master mind friend's brain for free and prevents this from becoming a problem.

18. Arrange for in-person meetings twice a year over a weekend, so your group has the luxury of bonding, doing a semi-annual review-preview, and discussing priorities in more depth.

Comedian Lily Tomlin said "Remember, we're all in this … alone."

Don't try to go it alone. You may eventually end up abandoning your idea – not because it doesn't have value, but because you just don't have the support that helps you persevere through the ups and downs and tough times.

This is true for almost any endeavor. An article in *USA TODAY* trumpeted, *U.S Marathoners Try Group Effort*. Reporter Dick Patrick reported that **U.S. runners are experiencing a resurgence in international competition, largely due to the fact they've started training in teams instead of in isolation.**

The tradition of the "lonely runner" takes a toll because you have to supply all your own discipline and motivation. Former Olympian Frank Shorter sponsors a group in Boulder, CO and is an advocate for the multi-faceted benefits of training together. He calls it "The Enclave Effect" and says "When you work together, everyone gets better. When someone breaks through and starts winning races, peers look at him and go, 'Hell, if he can do it, we can do it.'"

Are you tired of "going it alone," if you want the development of your idea to be fun and something you look forward to, pick up the phone and call a couple of kindred souls today. If you'd like to receive informed feedback from colleagues who have your best interests at heart, who can offer a "helicopter perspective" where they see things you can't, and who can provide "A rising tide raises all boats" motivation, use the techniques in this chapter to form your own IDEApreneur mastermind and creative enclave.

Questions to Ask – Actions to Take

1. Who has your back – and your front? Who can you turn to who you trust to give you support, informed feedback and encouragement to keep going? What do these people mean to you?
2. Do you have a formal master-mind or IDEApreneur support group to hold you accountable for making your idea a successful reality? How does that group work? How does it impact you?
3. Do you sometimes feel alone and isolated? Would you like to create a master-mind that feeds you energy so you don't have to supply all your own? Would you like to be connected with colleagues who keep you on track and moving forward? What steps from this chapter are you going to take to set that up? When? Where? How?

CHAPTER 26
Act on Your Ideas to Scale Your Influence and Income ... *for Good*

"My business is not to compare and compete – my business is to create." – **William Blake**

THIS LAST CHAPTER communicates my personal and professional approach to being an IDEApreneur.

We've talked about how you can increase your creativity, develop marketable ideas and monetize them through a variety of activities. Now, let's talk about developing a business philosophy that governs how you operate. If you commit to serving while selling and practicing "character in commerce," you can have the best of both worlds.

As you build your IDEApreneur career – please make sure your offering benefits others as much as it benefits you. If you do so, you create a type of corporate karma in which your clients and customers become word-of-mouth ambassadors who choose to recommend you to others because you can always be trusted to deliver win-win value.

If the point of view in the above paragraphs resonates with you, take responsibility for getting your idea out there. Don't give in to the "Who am I?" doubts that plague many people with an idea and a dream. Do you sometimes wonder, "Who am I to pursue this idea?" "Who am I to think I can be an inventor or innovator?"

As the saying goes, "All the wrong people have inferiority complexes." Are you feeling a little insecure about your idea? Or, maybe it's not you who's second-guessing your creative venture. Maybe you have a nay-saying significant other who is saying, "This will never work!" or "You're crazy!"

The next time anyone (including you) starts questioning whether you should pursue your dream, please remember Jana Wolff's story. It is a dramatic example that illustrates the importance of ACTING on your idea instead of letting fears and doubts talk you out of something that could make a difference for you and other people.

Jana Wolff was thinking about attending our very first Maui Writers Conference, but admitted she was having second thoughts. "I'm a little intimidated," she confessed. "I'm not sure I belong there."

"Why are you having second thoughts?" I asked.

"I keep thinking, 'Who am I to write a book? Who am I to tell people how to raise a child? It's like I'm putting myself up on a pedestal and saying, 'I know and you don't, and I'm going to tell you how to do it.' That's just not me," she sighed.

I told Jana, "The question to ask isn't, 'Am I perfect? Do I have it all together?' If that were the criteria for writing a book, no one would ever write one. What would happen if composers said, 'Why write a song about love, it's already been done?' or 'I can't write about love. I haven't figured it out yet.'"

"The question to ask is, 'Will people reading this ... benefit?' If our ideas will educate, enlighten, entertain, or inspire others; then not only do we have the right to write ... we have a responsibility to write."

Jana's eyebrows went up. "I never thought of it that way. You're right. Every time I dwell on my doubts, my confidence wilts. When I ask if someone reading my book will benefit, my confidence comes back."

Want good news? Jana finished her book *Secret Thoughts of an Adoptive Mother* … and kept her promise to tell what it's really like to be an adoptive parent. She and her husband Howard had adopted a bi-racial child. She had tried to find a resource to help them with some of the challenges they were experiencing, but couldn't find anything that talked honestly about the ups and downs of raising an adopted child.

For example, Jana had the courage to tell about the time they were having dinner and two year-old Ari picked up a hand full of spaghetti and threw it in her face. Her shocked reaction, "My son would never have done that" filled her with shame. She couldn't believe such a thought had even occurred to her. Jana admitted that she edited out the cute photos when sending pictures of Ari to his birth mother, because she was afraid Ari's birth-mother would see what a healthy, happy kid he was and want him back.

As a result of her honest sharing of what it's really like to be an adoptive parent (warts and all), Jana has received heartfelt thanks from thousands of people around the world who say, "Thank you for letting me know I'm not the only who has thought that, who has done that. Thank you for letting me know I'm not alone."

What's this mean for you? Think of it this way, **ideas in your head help no one**.

You can't make a difference for people with ideas you're going to develop – books you're going to write – businesses you're going to start. You can't make a living for yourself with creative projects you merely talk about.

Getting your ideas out of your mind and onto the page, onto the stage and online where people have an opportunity to benefit from them is a way to give back. It's a way to share what you've learned in the hopes it might save someone trial and terror learning. Turning an idea into a product, business or service that adds value is a way to contribute.

Next time you start dwelling on "Who am I?" doubts, remember Mae Sarton's inspiring words, "There is only one deprivation – and that is not be able to give one's gift." If you have been given an idea that could positively impact others, you have an obligation to stop procrastinating and start getting that gift, product, service, methodology out into the world. If you are coming from service not arrogance, then proceed. Doing so will set into motion a chain of events that could exceed your fondest hopes.

The Sundance Channel is running a fascinating series called *"Iconoclasts."* The show brings top artists, athletes, musicians, actors, directors, inventors and thought leaders together to discuss their work and the causes they care about. Grammy Award winning musician Alicia Keyes was featured recently and said something profound about how a single catalyst can spark a creative career.

Alicia said she'd been singing since she was four. When she started expressing an interest in piano, her family didn't have much money so it was difficult to pay for lessons, much less purchase a piano. "A friend ended up not needing his piano and gave it to us," she explained. She went on to say that when reporters ask what her biggest break was, she always says, "That piano."

In an ideal world, other people would initiate on our behalf and support our creativity. That doesn't always happen. Don't wait for others to "give" you permission (or a piano) to jump-start your IDEApreneur career. Be your own catalyst and create or join an Idea Accountability group so you don't have to go it alone.

I want to wrap up this book by sharing an inspirational example of the miracles (that's not too strong a word) that can happen when you commit to acting on your ideas and getting them out in the world.

Tom Tuohy, a lawyer in Chicago, was moved to start an organization called Dreams for Kids (www.DreamsForKids.org) that has helped more than 30,000 young people with disabilities get off the sidelines and into activities (sailing, golf, tennis, basketball, jet-skiing) they previously thought impossible.

Through serendipity (as mentioned before, what I now call SerenDestiny) I sat next to Tom at a conference luncheon. While finding out about each other, he told me the story of JJ O'Connor.

When JJ was 17, he was playing hockey and went into the boards at full speed. He broke his neck and became an instant quadriplegic. Following a series of surgeries and rehab, JJ started participating in Dreams for Kids programs and, on his 20th birthday, JJ told Tom he wanted to go to Mexico for spring break.

With his parents' permission, Tom and a friend fulfilled JJ's dream and they booked a trip to Cancun. On their final day, JJ wanted to swim with dolphins. Actually, he couldn't swim with them but he wanted to at least have the experience of getting in the water with them and being surrounded by these magnificent beings.

With Tom and Dick supporting JJ on either side, the trainer let a female dolphin into the lagoon. She circled the group and stopped right in front of JJ. She became rather agitated and the trainer guessed that her sonar had picked up that something was different about JJ's body. JJ, not wanting to "cause trouble," asked to be taken out of the pool.

Thankfully, the trainer persisted and said, "Let's bring in her boyfriend and see what happens." He let in the male dolphin who also circled the group and came to a halt in front of JJ and checked him out.

The two dolphins swam over to the far side the lagoon and conferred. Then, the female dolphin came back to JJ, stood up on her tail, leaned in, put her flippers on each side of JJ and gave him a kiss. As you can imagine, it was a magical moment for JJ and everyone else there.

Upon hearing this incredible story, I told Tom, "You've GOT to write this book."

He looked at me in surprise and asked, "What book?"

"*Kiss of a Dolphin,*" I said.

Tom did write that book. He said, "Never in my wildest dreams would I have considered writing a book. I was an attorney and busy running a non-profit. After that conversation, I realized that not only did I have the right to write, I had a responsibility to write."

Kiss of a Dolphin was launched at Chicago's Soldier Field (yes, where the Chicago Bears play football) with 1000 people (including JJ) in attendance. After seeing the impact Tom has on an audience, I asked him to share JJ's story as part of my closing keynote at the end of the 2006 Maui Writers Conference.

Based on his moving 4 minute (!) story, a participant in the audience named Jim Hayhurst approached Tom afterwards. Jim, a retired Top Gun test pilot, said, "I fly with a group called The Patriots, and we'd like you and JJ to come up with us at our next air show." So, Tom and JJ got to go up in a fighter jet at the Salinas Air Show in CA. The Patriots were so impressed with Tom and JJ, they changed their name to the DreamBirds.

A university dean finished reading *Kiss of a Dolphin* and turned to his wife and said, "We need to pledge our home to this fine organization." Their historic, million-dollar home will, someday be the center for even more programs for young people who deserve the same opportunities many of us take for granted.

Tom says, "Letters, emails and phone calls come in every single day from people around the world who have read Kiss of a Dolphin and been inspired to say "Hi" to people in wheelchairs instead of walking on by. That book, and JJ's story, have motivated them to volunteer for a nonprofit, appreciate how fortunate they are to have their mobility, and focus on what's right with their life."

He continued, "This is no longer just an idea…it's become a movement. And it never would have happened if the time had not been taken, the story had not been written, and the book not given as a gift to the world. Sam is fond of saying, 'Read it and reap.' I now know for a fact that if you write and speak on your idea and turn it into a tangible reality, you and many others will reap in ways you can't even begin to imagine."

In all my years of having the pleasure and privilege of helping individuals and organizations create one-of-a-kind ideas, I have never met anyone who regretted pursuing their dream, writing their book, starting their business or launching their IDEApreneur career…I have only met people who were sorry they didn't start sooner.

Follow the wise advice of Pope Paul who said, "The future starts today, not tomorrow" and Annie Dillard who said, "How we spend our days is, of course, how we spend our lives." Dig deep and discover your why, your purpose, and then start turning your idea into a money-making reality *today*.

Questions to Ask – Actions to Take

1. Who is an IDEApreneur you respect? Describe that person and why you admire him or her.
2. Create your own personal IDEApreneur Hall of Fame. When you are feeling discouraged, think about how they persevered through pushback, setbacks and the roller coaster ups and downs of turning an idea into a successful reality. Feed on their example for inspiration.

3. Do you have a favorite quote like the Leo Rosten quote that inspires you? Where are you going to post it to keep it top of mind so it helps you persevere all the way to prosperity?
4. Also post a vision of what you want to create. Whether it's the cover of a finished book, a homepage of a website, a picture of you on QVC, Shark Tank or Ellen or an announcement of your product launch or store opening; place that image where it's insight, in-mind so it stays top-of-mind.

Anytime you start losing hope or resolve, anytime you're even thinking of giving up ...

GAZE AT THAT VISUAL EVIDENCE OF WHAT IT WILL BE LIKE TO HAVE YOUR IDEA OUT IN THE WORLD MAKING A POSITIVE DIFFERENCE FOR OTHERS AND A PROSPEROUS DIFFERENCE FOR YOU.

And then begin again. Always, begin again.

Our world is better because of IDEApreneurs. Become one of them.

About the Author – Sam Horn

Sam Horn is the Founder/CEO of the Intrigue Agency which helps people design and deliver intriguing communications that get people's eyebrows UP.

She is on a mission to help people create the life, work and relationships of their dreams.

Her books – *Tongue Fu!®*, *POP!*, *IDEApreneur* and *Washington Post* bestseller **Got Your Attention?** have been featured in *New York Times, Forbes, INC, Investors Business Daily* and NPR.

Sam has had the privilege of speaking to more than half a million people worldwide and for such organizations as Boeing, Intel, Capital One, Cisco, Nationwide, National Geographic, and YPO.

Sam served as the Pitch Coach for Springboard Enterprises which has helped entrepreneurs receive $8.8 billion (yes, that's a B) in funding.

Sam co-founded the Business Book Festival (held at USA Today headquarters) and served as the Executive Director of the world-renowned Maui Writers Conference for 17 years where she worked with the publishing industry's top agents, editors, authors and screenwriters.

She has helped hundreds of people create one-of-a-kind books, brands, TEDx talks, funding pitches and high-stakes presentations that added value for all involved.

A partial list of clients includes Terry Jones, Founder of Travelocity, Nell Merlino, founder of Take Your Daughter to Work Day, Larry Lynch, former Director of the Disney Institute and Sandra Joseph, who played the lead role of Christine in Broadway's Phantom of the Opera for ten years.

Sam's newest book **SOMEDAY is *not a Day in the Week*** shares stories and insights from her Year by the Water on how to make the rest of our life the best of our life.

It features questionnaires and interactive exercises that help readers get crystal clear about what really matters so they can bring more of that into their life starting today, not someday.

The book has been featured on Harvard Business Review's Ascend site, on JLD's top-ranked Entrepreneur on Fire podcast, and has received glowing reviews from Library Journal and Booklist.

Sheri Salata (Former Executive Producer of The Oprah Winfrey Show) calls Sam "one of the bright lights and most accessible wisdom-sharers in our culture today."

www.INTRIGUEagency.com

Want to Work with Sam?

SPEAKING: Arrange for Sam Horn to share these *IDEApreneur* techniques at your conference. Discover for yourself why audiences rave about Sam's inspiring, interactive programs that have everyone connecting, contributing and instantly applying these insights to their priorities.

CONSULTNG: Contact us to describe your idea, your goals, your current status to explore how Sam and her Intrigue Agency team can help you turn it into a profitable reality.

MEDIA: Interview Sam for your TV show, newspaper, magazine, book club, podcast or radio show. You can trust Sam to deliver intriguing insights, inspiring stories and innovative suggestions your viewers and readers can use immediately to produce real-world results.

SOCIAL MEDIA: Connect with Sam online to receive curated IDEApreneurs best practices, compelling quotes, and relevant research that will contribute to your success. Twitter = @SamHornIntrigue, Facebook = www.facebook.com/SamHornIntrigue,

Blog = www.INTRIGUEagency.com

Contact Cheri Grimm at 1 805 528-4351 or
Cheri@INTRIGUEagency.com

www.ingramcontent.com/pod-product-compliance
Lightning Source LLC
Chambersburg PA
CBHW060519080526
44586CB00012B/535